Understanding Preschooler Development

Other Books in This Series:
Understanding Infant Development
Understanding Toddler Development

Understanding
Preschooler
Development

Margaret B. Puckett & Janet K. Black

with Joseph M. Moriarity

Redleaf Press
www.redleafpress.org
800-423-8309

Published by Redleaf Press
a division of Resources for Child Caring
10 Yorkton Court
St. Paul, MN 55117
Visit us online at www.redleafpress.org.

First edition 2007
Cover photograph by Steve Wewerka
Interior typeset in Janson Text
Interior illustrations by Chris Wold Dyrud
Printed in Canada
14 13 12 11 10 09 08 07   1 2 3 4 5 6 7 8

Redleaf Press books are available at a special discount when purchased in bulk for special premiums and sales promotions. For details, contact the sales manager at 800-423-8309.

Library of Congress Cataloging-in-Publication Data
Puckett, Margaret B.
    Understanding preschooler development / Margaret B. Puckett and Janet K. Black with Joseph M. Moriarity. -- 1st ed.
        p. cm.
    Includes bibliographical references and index.
    ISBN 978-1-933653-03-7
    1. Child development. 2. Preschool children. I. Black, Janet K. II. Moriarity, Joseph M. III. Title.
    HQ767.9.P83 2006
    305.231--dc22
                                        2006038904

Printed on acid-free paper.

Understanding Preschooler Development

Introduction

Whether you are a parent or early childhood professional, you know that caring for and raising children are rewarding challenges: They represent the best of times and the worst of times—sometimes at virtually the same time!

Raising children in the United States has become even more difficult over the last few decades. Parents work more hours, commute farther, are more stressed, and have less free time now than ever before. The media and our consumer culture do not always act in the best interests of our children. Ads targeted directly at even very young children constantly promote unhealthy foods as well as toys and games of questionable value. Much of the entertainment that popular media offers is violent—even those shows supposedly designed for children—and more than a thousand studies have shown that movie and television violence fosters real violence.

At the same time, parents and other caregivers have more accurate information available to them—now more than ever before—about how children develop and about how adults can support their growth and development. This knowledge is important for those who interact with, care for, and provide educational experiences to infants and young children.

By the beginning of their fourth year, children have taken huge steps in all areas of development: sensory, physical/motor, social, emotional, cognitive, and language. The most obvious change parents and child care professionals may see is in preschoolers' physical growth and the range of new motor skills they develop. When compared with two- or three-year-olds, preschoolers are taller, faster, stronger, more agile, and much better coordinated. Along with this physical development come remarkable advances in their social abilities; in their reading, language, and communication skills; and in their desire and ability to be more independent.

This book is designed to be both a text and a kind of manual for working with children. As you read and study this and the other books in this series, you'll learn up-to-date information about a number of areas, including the following:

- the expected patterns of physical and motor development in children ages four through five
- developmental landmarks in large- and small-muscle development
- perceptual-motor development
- body and gender awareness; gender identity and gender role development
- neurological and psychosocial development
- major factors influencing physical and motor development
- social and moral development, and the factors that influence them
- health and well-being
- strategies for enhancing physical, motor, and perceptual-motor development

You'll also discover that recent research has challenged many traditional theories of how to best support children's growth and development. What is important in the end is that the theories and research presented here help parents and early childhood professionals improve the quality of life and education for children in their care.

Part One

Physical and Motor Development

The first and foremost thing you can expect of a child is that he is a child.

—Armin Grams

A secure, healthful and nourishing environment is a child's basic right.

—Convention on the Rights of the Child

During infancy, children are relatively helpless. They are just beginning to communicate with others and explore their environments. During the toddler years, children become more independent, both physically and cognitively. In the preschooler stage, ages four and five, children's maturing brains and growing bodies help them take a huge leap in cognitive and physical abilities. They're old enough to take some responsibility for their physical well-being.

A number of factors influence this physical and motor development—genetic makeup, good nutrition, healthy routines, and safety. Part 1 examines typical patterns of physical and motor development in preschoolers and identifies the developmental landmarks in large- and small-muscle development. Newfound large-muscle coordination helps preschoolers balance, hop, jump, climb, slide, gallop, skip, and more. Advances in small-motor control help them dress and undress with efficiency as well as use crayons, paintbrushes, beads and string, pegs and pegboards, and other small objects.

Child care programs can promote physical and motor development and cognitive development by providing activities that encourage movement, manipulation, and social interaction. You'll see why children who don't master early sensory, perceptual, and motor skills may have difficulty with more complicated thinking and reasoning problems later in school.

Safety becomes a critical issue for child care professionals caring for four- and five-year-olds. This book presents important information on playground safety and selecting appropriate toys, as well as on preventing burns, choking, poisoning, drowning, and accidents in general. You'll also explore why child development experts are expressing concern about the effects on children of spending an increasing amount of time in nonparental care.

Physical and Motor Competence

Theories of Development

Children seemingly come into the world as blank slates, but in fact the slate isn't completely clean. Anyone who has raised or cared for young children recognizes that, at a very early age, young children's abilities and personalities differ from one another—even from their siblings. By the time they reach age four, they are clearly their own person, with likes and dislikes, a distinct personality, and rapidly growing abilities.

Child development researchers have long debated the question of how much of our personality and our abilities is inherited (nature) and how much is affected by how we are raised (nurture). They have created a number of theories about how growth happens, what causes us to behave in certain ways, and how and why we have some abilities and talents but not others.

Some researchers and child psychologists think that growth and development are controlled mainly by heredity, that we are born with a kind of blueprint that defines what, when, and how much each aspect of growth and development will happen. This is called the *maturationist* theory of development.

Other researchers and theorists believe that the environment in which we grow up plays a much more important role in our development and growth. According to this theory, called *behaviorism*, our family life and culture shape the kind of adult we will become much more than our genes.

Another theory, *developmental interaction*, takes a different view. It says that children are born with certain abilities that can blossom when supported by a rich and stimulating environment—or impaired by an environment lacking mental stimulation and rewards.

Still other theorists and educators suggest a *transactional perspective*, in which a person's inherited traits and environmental experiences affect each other through regular interactions. Thus inherited traits are shaped by experience and experience is shaped by inherited traits.

Perhaps the most prominent theory of child growth, development, and learning today—the *systems approach*—proposes that a variety of influences affect who we become. These influences include biology, race, ethnicity, cultural and religious values, tradition, gender, financial status, and others.

Although humans are genetically programmed for coordination, movement, and mobility, environmental differences in early childhood can mean that preschoolers begin developing and mastering various motor abilities—riding a tricycle, catching a ball, skipping—at different times. Such differences are neither good nor bad, normal nor abnormal.

General Physical Characteristics

From conception to six months of age, an infant grows dramatically. During the toddler and preschool stages, growth rates tend to slow (they move at a steady pace until puberty). Children ages four and five commonly grow two-and-a-half to three-and-a-half inches in height and gain four to five pounds each year until around age six. These stages of growth are fairly predictable, although the rates are influenced by genetic makeup and environment. How tall, heavy, or well coordinated a child is (or will become) depends on genetics, health history, nutrition, psychosocial well-being, and number of opportunities for physical and motor activity.

During the preschooler stage, body proportions change from the chunky, top-heavy build of the toddler to a leaner, more upright look. The child's head, which was one-fourth of the total body length at age two, is about one-sixth of the total body length at age five to five-and-a-half. The brain reaches 90 percent of its adult weight by age five, and the maturing of nerve connections (axons and dendrites) is fairly complete, making more complex motor abilities possible.

Boys and girls at this stage have similar physiques, and you'll notice that their "baby fat" is being replaced with more bone and muscle. For reasons we don't fully understand, boys tend to gain more muscle at this age, while girls tend to retain more fat. For both boys and girls, though, changing body proportions result in a larger chest circumference and a flatter stomach, longer arms and legs, and feet that have lost the fatty look of baby feet.

Regular health assessments during these growing years monitor height and weight gains, providing preliminary information about a child's overall health and nutritional status. Children whose measurements are in the top or bottom 5 percent, or whose measurements show major change from one assessment to the next, may have health or nutritional concerns that require further evaluation. (In some cases, growth spurts occur. For instance, after a long illness, the body's catch-up mechanisms come into play and speed the growth process for a period of time until the body reaches the size it would have attained had the illness not occurred.) It's important for child care professionals to look for unusual growth patterns because they can indicate possible health problems such as overnutrition or undernutrition; endocrine disorders such as hyperthyroidism or hypo-thyroidism; growth hormone imbalance; disease; dehydration; fluid retention; and more.

Large-Motor Development

By ages four and five, children are very active. Now that they have mastered walking and running, their movements are expansive and include large-muscle coordination that helps with balancing, hopping, jumping, climbing, sliding, galloping, skipping, and more. The following table shows typical large-motor skills at ages four and five.

Age Four	Age Five
Rides a tricycle	Rides a bicycle (may need training wheels)
Climbs stairs with alternating feet	Descends stairs with alternating feet
Balances on one foot for a short period	Balances on one foot for a count of 5 to 10
Climbs playground equipment with agility	Experiments with playground climbing equipment
Enjoys creative responses to music	Enjoys learning simple rhythms and movement routines
Skips on one foot	Skips with both feet
Jumps easily in place	Hops on one foot in place

Throws a ball	Catches a ball
Likes to chase	Enjoys follow-the-leader
Walks a straight line marked on the floor	Walks a low, wide kindergarten balance beam
Enjoys noncompetitive games	Enjoys noncompetitive games

Large-motor control and coordination is important because it enhances the child's development in all other areas:

- overall health and vitality
- cognitive development—children are better able to explore the world around them
- psychosocial development—children's independence, self-sufficiency, self-image, and self-confidence are enhanced

As you will see in later chapters, children with a positive self-image and strong self-confidence also have more successful interactions with others.

A large part of the day should be set aside for preschoolers to use, expand, and refine their large-motor coordination. Regular large-motor activities lead to better physical fitness, which is made up of two components. *Health-related fitness* includes muscular strength, muscular endurance, flexibility, and heart-lung endurance. *Performance-related fitness* includes balance, coordination, agility, speed, and power. Both types are essential to healthy, sturdy, well-coordinated bodies, and promote bone growth in young children. In addition, healthy motor development plays a vital role in perceptual-motor development and learning.

Young children's "work" is play—in the case of preschoolers, *active* play—in which they use their whole bodies (as opposed to passive activities such as watching television or playing on a computer or Game Boy).

Small-Motor Development

As preschoolers get better at controlling their large muscles, their small muscles also become more developed. As a result, they become better able to do precise activities and small-motor tasks. The following table shows typical small-motor skills at ages four and five.

Age Four	Age Five
Exhibits self-help skills in dressing: some difficulty with zippers, small buttons, tying shoes	Dresses with ease Ties shoes
Works a puzzle of several pieces	Enjoys puzzles with many pieces
Exhibits right- or left-handedness; occasional ambidextrous behaviors	Exhibits right- or left-handedness
Enjoys crayons, paint, clay, and other art media	Enjoys drawing, painting, and using a variety of writing tools
Uses beads and strings, snap blocks, and various manipulative toys	Enjoys a variety of manipulative and construction-type toys

The ability to perform small-motor tasks becomes possible through the emergence and maturation of *prehension* (the coordination of fingers and thumb to permit grasping) and *dexterity* (quick, precise movement and coordination of the hands and fingers). By age five, children's improving prehension abilities let them use crayons, paintbrushes, beads and strings, pegs and pegboards, and other small objects, and to manage dressing and undressing with efficiency. Children also gain the dexterity they need to put small puzzle pieces into place; to close fasteners (small buttons, zippers, etc.); to sort playing cards; and to write understandable letters and numerals, though this skill may be less advanced.

Dexterity depends on a neurological process in which certain abilities become located in the left or right hemisphere of the brain. Becoming right-handed or left-handed is part of this developmental process, which begins in infancy when children show a preference for a left- or right-facing sleeping position. Foot preference is fairly well established from ages three to five years, though it sometimes takes longer to emerge.

"Handedness," whether right or left, helps children develop and use their growing small-motor abilities. Some preschoolers use both hands with ease; some use one hand for one activity, such as eating, and the other for another activity, such as throwing or reaching. This process is controlled by complex neurological connections in the brain and needs no encouragement. A child's hand preference may not be fully established until six, seven, or eight years of age.

Perceptual-Motor Development

THE STORY OF TWO FAMILIES

In the first two books in this series, Understanding Infant Development *and* Understanding Toddler Development, *we introduced two children, Angela and Jeremy, and their caretakers. Jeremy came into the world as a healthy baby under excellent conditions and with mature parents. Angela was not as fortunate, having been born prematurely to a young, inexperienced mother. The story of Jeremy and Angela's development as preschoolers continues in this book.*

Angela has just awakened from her afternoon nap. Hearing the voice of her grandmother across the room chatting with her teacher, she is further aroused. She sits up, rubs her eyes, clumsily retrieves her shoes, and makes her way toward her grandmother's voice. Once there, Angela is greeted by her grandmother with hugs and questions about her day.

Angela has just demonstrated a simple *perceptual-motor* sequence that involved hearing a sound (auditory sensation), recognizing and identifying the sound as that of her grandmother's voice (perception), and making a decision to walk toward the source of the sound (locomotion).

Definition: *Perceptual-motor development*—the relationship between a sensory experience and a motor response.

We come into the world equipped with sensory abilities: touch, sight, hearing, smell, taste, and *kinesthesis*. Our sense organs provide information about what is going on around us and within us. The ability to make sense of these sensations—to understand them—is called *perception*.

Definition: *Kinesthesis*—the sensation of our body's presence, position, and movement.

Our perception depends on our sense organs and kinesthetic abilities combined with our cognitive development and experience. Once we notice a sensation, we have to decide what to do with that information, which usually means an action, for example, turning toward a sound, placing a hand over your eyes to shield them from a bright light, or reaching for an object. This relationship between sensory experience and motor response is called perceptual-motor development. Perceptual-motor skills help our cognitive abilities, body awareness, space and directional awareness, and time-space orientation.

Children develop their perceptual-motor skills through activities that encourage them to explore, experiment, and manipulate. Therefore it is very important that early childhood classrooms include a variety of sensory activities, for instance, matching fragrance containers (sense of smell), mixing and matching fabric patterns (sight) or textures (touch), and cooking (taste). Musical and rhythmic activities combine auditory and motor abilities as children respond to such elements as space, tempo, and volume.

> *Children develop their perceptual-motor skills through activities that encourage them to explore, experiment, and manipulate.*

Children who do not master early sensory, perceptual, and motor skills can have difficulty with more complicated thinking and reasoning problems in later school years. For example, a child must have the ability to perceive shapes in order to be able to learn to form letters and numbers. Children must rely on sensory, motor, and perceptual abilities to respond well to tone of voice as a clue to another's message, and to be able to interpret other people's facial and body language.

Body Awareness, Movement, and Simple Games

As young children master basic locomotor skills, they begin to develop an awareness of their bodies. This awareness includes not just the names and locations of body parts and what children can make them do, but also a growing sense that all body parts are interconnected and that bodies have both abilities and limitations. Body awareness grows out of children's visual, auditory, tactile, and kinesthetic perceptions. Although as adults we rarely think about it, our ability to move from place to place without running into people or stumbling over objects depends on the coordination of our vision, hearing, touch, and kinesthetic perception. People's body awareness is also influenced by their feelings—either positive or negative—about their physical characteristics and capabilities.

Body awareness is a powerful force in all aspects of development: perceptual-motor, psychosocial, and cognitive. It becomes part of children's emerging sense of self, and it affects their feelings of competence. Body awareness and confidence give children both a sense of control and the motivation they need to try more and more complex physical/motor activities.

Movement activities and simple games help coordinate and refine basic body movements and support the development of more complex motor abilities. Four- and five-year-olds especially enjoy movement activities and simple games. They enjoy responding to music in spontaneous and creative ways, pantomiming, playing follow-the-leader, and playing catch. Balancing or hopping on one foot, jumping over obstacles, and walking a balance beam forward, sideways, and backward can be challenging and self-affirming activities.

Child care programs that encourage physical and motor development meet children's needs for movement, for manipulation, and for social interactions and pretend play. To promote overall health and physical development, each child's day should include ample opportunity for movement, including creative movement, dance, and the use of equipment that requires large-motor coordination. Outdoor play should also be a daily event and should include activities that incorporate running, jumping, skipping, and other large-motor skills that help build physical fitness.

> *Because children need to be physically active, it is not only difficult for a caregiver to keep children quiet and still for long periods of time, it is actually unhealthy for the children.*

According to a 2006 Kaiser Foundation study that looked at media use among the very young, children age six and under spend an average of two hours a day playing video games, using computers, and watching television and videos. This is basically the same amount of time they spent in outdoor activities and two-and-a-half times the average forty-eight minutes spent reading or being read to. Studies in the past have linked prolonged television viewing to childhood obesity, poor sleep patterns, and later adult violence.

Because children *need* to be physically active, it is not only difficult for a caregiver to keep children quiet and still for long periods of time, it is actually unhealthy for the children. Preschool and kindergarten programs that require children to sit or to work at tables or desks and listen to teacher-directed lessons for extended periods of time are developmentally inappropriate because they limit children's opportunities for more lively and valuable activities.

> *Jeremy and his friends Caitlin, DeLisa, Jared, and Mac have decided to play a racing game to see how fast they can run to the "faraway" tree on their kindergarten playground. They decide that Jeremy will tell them when to go. After he counts to three and shouts "Go!" the five of them run off. DeLisa, who is slightly taller and heavier than her companions and who is quick and athletic, is the first off, followed by Caitlin, who has well-coordinated large-muscle control, though she is somewhat shorter than the rest of the children. Caitlin is followed by Mac, who is in the eightieth percentile for height for boys of his age, though he is thin and only in the fortieth percentile for weight. Mac is followed in the race by Jared and Jeremy, who are*

both in the fiftieth percentile for height and weight, with average motor coordination and abilities.

The five run with energy and power. Jared stumbles and falls, scraping his knees; he leaves the race crying and looking for a teacher. Jeremy tries to catch up with the others. DeLisa steps out of the race, panting and breathless. Caitlin, short and fast, and Mac, with his long stride, arrive at the tree at the same time. Both proclaim themselves the winner. An argument ensues, unfriendly words are exchanged, and Caitlin announces she is going to tell the teacher. Jeremy, in the meantime, fights back tears. The game was his idea, after all, and he expected to win. Disappointed at losing, he joins DeLisa, and the two decide they are not going to play with Mac and Caitlin anymore.

As the story illustrates, children in competition experience advantage or disadvantage at times due to the wide range in their physical/motor abilities, size, body type, and experience. While physically active games are enjoyable for young children when they are simple and, for the most part, created by them, they often find actual competition frustrating, defeating, and unrewarding.

Games created by children characteristically involve spontaneously created rules. Creating a game, creating the rules, trying to make them fair, picking "even" teams, and calling out players who try to cheat all help in children's social and moral development (something we'll examine in later chapters). In this way, games serve important psychosocial functions in child development; they encourage and enhance children's physical and moral well-being.

The importance of child-created games raises questions about the current situation in the United States in which so many young children are involved in sports that are organized, coached, and refereed by adults. Children naturally invent games. Giving them the opportunity to do so and to deal with the issues that come up allows them to learn about fair play and cooperation and to develop effective problem-solving skills in a way that adult-run games do not. Adults *can* offer an advantage in child care settings, however: They can gently guide games toward outcomes that are enjoyable for every participant.

Chapter 1 examined physical development, large- and small-motor development, increasing body and gender awareness, new locomotor skills, and the importance of opportunities to interact, explore, and play with peers. The next chapter explores the relationship between physical/motor development and psychosocial/cognitive development. You'll learn more about the important connection between preschoolers' self-concept and their general awareness of physical characteristics and abilities. You'll see how their growing abilities give them new opportunities to learn about the world around them and to help them begin taking responsibility for their own health and safety.

2 The Relationship between Physical/Motor and Psychosocial/Cognitive Development

Between ages four and five, a child's physical growth and development allow him to move, play, explore, and interact more with others. These experiences spur the development of new social skills and cognitive abilities.

Psychosocial Development

At ages four and five, a child's self-concept is closely connected to awareness of physical characteristics (hair, eye, and skin color; physical abilities; gender; and so on). Young children's physical characteristics and emerging abilities also affect their interactions with others. These interactions provide positive and/or negative feedback, which play an important role in their growing self-concept. A child who is viewed as physically or socially attractive, for example, may receive different feedback than a child who is viewed as unattractive or difficult. Similarly, a child who is seen by others as having unusual features, such as particular hair, eye, or skin color; freckles or dimples; physical grace and poise; or other noticeable features, often receives quite a bit of attention. That attention, even if it's positive and complimentary, may be unwelcome to the child and can influence her self-image and interactions with others. Perhaps you remember a family event at this age when you became the center of attention because of some funny or cute thing you did and felt embarrassed or uncomfortable. Preschoolers can be particularly sensitive to others' comments. Their self-image and self-confidence can be influenced in both subtle and obvious ways.

This point is particularly important for young children with special needs, who sometimes have difficulty accepting and being accepted by others. Helping these children develop their physical and motor abilities and their self-help skills to the utmost is very important because developing these skills builds confidence and can motivate further effort and practice. Improved skills also promote self-esteem. When children feel accepted, appreciated, and self-confident, and when they enjoy control over their bodies, their interpersonal relationships are enhanced. For more information on psychosocial development, see part 2.

> *When children feel accepted, appreciated, and self-confident, and when they enjoy control over their bodies, their interpersonal relationships are enhanced.*

Cognitive Development

Preschoolers' growing physical and motor capabilities expand what they can do and where they can go, giving them new opportunities to explore the world around them and supporting their cognitive development. Taking a trip to a farm for a pony ride; helping with appropriate household chores; moving and dancing to music; reading; helping a parent wash the family car; taking more responsibility for their health, safety, and cleanliness; and being part of family discussions about household safety and health rules are some of the many activities that help connect preschoolers' physical and motor development to their cognitive development. You'll learn more about cognitive development in part 3.

Learning to Be Responsible for One's Own Health and Safety

By the time children reach ages four and five, they're beginning to understand the importance of health-related concepts such as eating, sleeping, resting, and exercise; they're old enough to learn some responsibility for themselves. While we can't expect young children to protect themselves without adult supervision, teaching, and encouragement, parents and caregivers can encourage them to cooperate in a number of areas, including the following:

- regular teeth-brushing, frequent hand-washing, and other hygienic practices
- predictable naptime and bedtime routines
- understanding the need for nutritious food over junk food

- appreciating the need for regular medical and dental checkups and immunizations
- recognizing potential hazards (hot items, electrical items, poisons, unsafe toys, playground and environmental hazards, streets, driveways, and traffic dangers)
- obeying household and family rules (regarding television usage and acceptable program content, choice of computer activities and electronic games, appropriate time and place for certain behaviors and activities)
- consistently using vehicle safety seats or restraints
- answering the phone or door as instructed
- understanding where to safely play with certain items, such as tricycles or other wheeled toys, and understanding which toys or equipment require adult help
- learning their full name, address (with ZIP code), phone number (with area code), parent's name(s) and cell or work phone numbers, how to call for help, and so on

Responsibility for personal health and safety emerges slowly and irregularly over many years. Although abilities and sense of responsibility are growing in four- and five-year-olds, the adults in their lives must still be responsible for providing continuing and careful supervision and protection. It is easy to assume that young children are more capable in these areas than they actually are, but if you pay close attention, you'll see that their behaviors are at best inconsistent. This is because four- and five-year-olds still have limited long-term memory and limited or irregular chances to practice these skills. They're easily distracted; they can quickly find more exciting things to do; and they're always eager to explore and learn about new things. In addition, their caregivers may not have set up consistent routines and expectations. The major responsibility for providing safe, hygienic environments and developmentally appropriate experiences remains with caregivers. Moreover, adults continue to be children's most powerful role models.

Gender Awareness and Gender Constancy

By age three, young children show gender awareness and identity by correctly labeling themselves and others as "boys" or "girls." However, *gender constancy*—understanding that gender stays the same regardless of age, clothing, hairstyle, or individual wishes—doesn't begin to appear until between ages five and seven. Development of gender constancy seems to follow a pattern: first, realizing that one's own gender won't change; second, realizing that others of the same gender will stay the same; and finally, realizing that others of the opposite gender will stay the same.

Understanding the idea of gender constancy brings a growing awareness that boys and girls, and men and women, differ in a number of ways, including anatomy. As children begin to realize that anatomy, rather than other factors such as clothes or hairstyle, defines gender, they become more interested in the human body. Young children are curious about the physiological differences between boys and girls and between men and women. They watch and compare the anatomies and behaviors of each, forming ideas, sometimes stereotypical, about male and female bodies, roles, and behavior. They imitate male and female behaviors in their play, and they experiment with being male and female.

Some behaviors embarrass or worry caregivers—such as when children ask direct questions about body parts and functions, giggle about and tease members of the opposite sex, engage in "bathroom talk" or "playing doctor." However, these are normal behaviors that simply show that children have a growing awareness of the differences between genders. As a child care professional, it's important that your response to such behavior is positive, informative, and age-appropriate. It should help children feel more comfortable and satisfied with their gender identity. Acting shocked or embarrassed or ignoring questions is unhelpful. Children need honest, simple, and direct answers, and they must feel comfortable and safe asking questions as they think of them. By providing accurate labels, discussing gender roles and behaviors, setting examples, and modeling healthy gender identity and self-acceptance, you can help children build accurate and positive self-concepts. As children begin to understand gender constancy, they become very interested in gender-role behaviors and pay particularly close attention to gender role models.

In the next chapter, you'll learn more about some of the factors, both inherited and environmental, that influence physical and motor development.

3 Factors Influencing Physical and Motor Development

A variety of factors—including genetics, hygiene and health, nutrition, and safety—affect your children's physical and motor development. Most of these factors are directly influenced by the quality of care provided in child care settings.

Genetic Makeup

Genes control a child's rate of development, affecting everything from when motor abilities emerge to when growth spurts occur, teeth break through, and when children reach their adult height. We all have inherited a genetic blueprint from our parents. This blueprint determines such characteristics as gender, blood type, skin color, hair color and texture, eye color, potential height, temperament, and other characteristics that make each person unique. Optimal development depends on healthy genetic traits and supportive, healthy environments.

Because each child grows at his own pace, comparisons with siblings or peers can be misleading. Each child's growth happens according to the child's biological blueprint and his unique experiences and interactions with the environment. Adults should be aware of their expectations and their reactions to children's developmental accomplishments. A parent or teacher who shows disappointment when a child fails to master a task (for example, using scissors, catching a ball, or writing letters correctly) may be putting unfair expectations on the child because she simply hasn't reached the needed biological maturity for mastery. Being too proud of developmental accomplishments that the child has no control over is also misleading. The child is simply showing the results of genetic traits over which she has no conscious control.

Genetics are clearly not the only factor involved in this process. Interactions between heredity and environment affect when certain attributes and skills appear. Height and weight, for instance, depend on nutrition and other health factors. Motor coordination depends on opportunities to move about, explore, discover, and practice new abilities. Certain personality characteristics that might seem inherited—such as energy level, fearfulness, and sociability—are actually affected by interactions with others. Adequate health care, proper nutrition, avoidance of accidents and stress, appropriate expectations, and sociocultural factors all play a role in how a child's genetic traits emerge. Individuals come into the world with blueprints for development, but actual development is connected to, and depends on, environmental influences.

Hygiene: Preventing the Spread of Disease among Children in Groups

Today, four- and five-year-olds attending preschool, child care, and kindergarten programs, as well as those enrolled in before- and/or after-school programs, are exposed to a variety of illnesses. Common infectious diseases include conjunctivitis (pink eye), lice, scabies, impetigo, ear infections, colds, flu, and a variety of upper-lung conditions. They are also at greater risk for contracting intestinal infections that cause diarrhea. Because childhood illnesses can be so infectious, it's important to watch them for signs of illness or infection.

At a child care center, children share almost everything: tabletops, toys, sinks, shelving and other furnishings, and toileting areas. In addition, young children like to share food using unwashed hands. Unless staff take appropriate safety steps, the spread of disease is almost impossible to avoid. To prevent the spread of diseases and infections, staff should establish routines and behaviors that include the following:

- frequent and thorough handwashing with soap and warm water
- teaching children proper handwashing techniques and requiring handwashing after toileting, before and after eating, after coughing or sneezing, and at other appropriate times
- cleaning toys, changing tables, and play surfaces with a disinfecting solution (either a commercial solution or a mixture of one-fourth cup of bleach to one gallon of water)

- wearing gloves when cleaning areas contaminated with blood, vomit, or other bodily fluids
- watching children for signs or symptoms of illness, and then isolating an ill child until a parent can be summoned
- providing nutritious foods, snacks, beverages, and fresh drinking water
- keeping healthy, predictable schedules for meals, snacks, rest, and play

Healthy Routines

Predictable routines are important for good health and a sense of well-being. Plan daily schedules to include regular meal, snack, rest, and activity times; whenever possible, give children a number of activity choices.

Children appreciate having both quiet and active times throughout the day. This helps them avoid getting overtired or overstimulated. Though four- and five-year-olds seem to have an endless supply of energy, they actually tire quickly. Of course, they can recover quite quickly after a short rest period too. Quiet times that include soft conversation, story reading, short naps, or quiet play can help make a preschooler's day healthier and happier.

Nutrition

Children's diets must include enough nutrients to meet the needs of growing bones and muscles, promote healthy permanent teeth, and maintain growth and development of all body tissues and organs. Preschoolers need a lot of energy to maintain high activity levels, and more active children may need more food than less active ones of the same age and size.

While fulfilling their responsibility for providing nutritious and adequate diets for the children they care for, adults can take several steps to help children develop the good eating and nutrition habits that are important to healthy growth. These include establishing regular eating times, avoiding snacks that are high in calories but low in nutrients, and helping children get enough daily exercise and activity.

A number of serious concerns about nutrition have blossomed in the past few years, including:

- a large and dangerous increase in obesity among Americans in general and among young children in particular

- a change in what Americans eat—more high-fat, high-calorie fast foods and fewer fresh vegetables, fruits, and whole grains
- an overabundance of high-calorie, low-nutrition snacks
- an increase in food-related allergies and nutrition-related illnesses among children, including high cholesterol levels, diabetes, and high blood pressure

Additionally, a growing number of health problems are related to poor nutrition, including poor growth and development and a higher chance of illness, emotional problems, and learning disabilities.

ADULT INFLUENCES ON CHILDREN'S EATING HABITS

Four- and five-year-olds are now ripe for developing good eating habits. They're old enough to have some understanding of nutrition and its effect on their bodies, and more important, they are beginning to make their own food choices and form their own eating patterns. Child care professionals can play an important role in helping children learn how to make good food choices, including avoiding high-fat, high-sugar, low-nutrient foods. You can have short discussions about how many of the foods that are advertised in magazines, in junk mail, on billboards, and on television do not make people healthier; this can help counter the effect of advertising and encourage children to make better choices. Children can be taught about what makes a balanced diet and can help in planning meals and snacks. When young children participate in this way, they begin to understand the importance of good nutrition and may develop more nutritious food preferences. Learning to make good choices about food at an early age is a powerful defense against risky food behaviors (which often become habits) and food-related illnesses.

FOOD PREFERENCES

Preschoolers are beginning to make the transition to more adultlike eating habits. However, they have not developed a taste for a wide variety of foods, especially vegetables, so it's important to give them a number of food choices—particularly ones that have many nutrients.

As children get older, they begin to have strong food preferences and dislikes. Parents and child care professionals naturally want to provide adequate and nutritious meals and snacks for preschool children, but they are often puzzled when children show little interest in, or even dislike for, some foods. There are developmental reasons for many of these behaviors.

CHILDHOOD FOOD PREFERENCES ARE AFFECTED BY THE FOLLOWING:

- Cultural practices and preferences
- Peer and sibling influences
- Television and other media advertising
- Naturally occurring fluctuations in the child's interest in certain foods
- The child's ability to manage the food—using utensils, ease of chewing and swallowing
- Food allergies
- A temporary dislike of certain foods connected to an unpleasant experience (being reprimanded or embarrassed at a time when eating the food; an illness associated with a food; the same food served too often)
- Connecting food with a particularly pleasant memory (eating at a grandparent's or a friend's house; a special occasion; a holiday dinner)
- Liking (or disliking) food because of its temperature, texture, color, smell, or serving size; compatibility with other foods on the plate; cleanliness of silverware, dishes, and eating surfaces
- Parental pressure to eat certain foods or to "clean your plate"

The eating behaviors of young children show their changing growth patterns as well as their physiological and psychological needs. Children at ages four and five are growing less quickly than in previous years and thus need less food. Their new food preferences show their growing ability to recognize different tastes, their desire to make choices, and their growing sense of independence, both at home and in other settings. The ability to choose from a number of foods and snacks supports their growing sense of self-reliance and control. Of course, the ability to recognize different tastes also means that preschoolers can become very stubborn about what they will and won't eat!

Researchers have found that a number of childhood experiences influence what and how much children choose to eat. Being aware of these factors may help you in planning meals at a child care center and in working with children who have varying food preferences:

- Food preferences are a response to a combination of factors involving a food's taste, smell, appearance, and/or texture. These preferences change over time as children experience more types of foods and different spices.
- A child's cultural environment shapes his acceptance of different foods.
- Generally, infants and young children do not quickly accept new foods unless they are sweet.
- As exposure to a new food increases, a child's preference for it also increases. Often children must be exposed to a new food as many as ten times before acceptance is achieved; of course, in some cases, they will never like it.
- When foods are given to children in a comfortable environment, their preferences for those foods are stronger; however, when children are forced to eat certain foods to obtain rewards, they may grow to dislike those foods.
- Children seem to instinctively prefer high-energy foods.
- Children may have the ability to intuitively regulate how much they eat based on the calorie content of the food they have eaten over a number of meals. To determine how much to eat, they rely more on this physiological sense of calorie intake than adults do.
- Research says that while the amount of food consumed can vary highly from meal to meal, children's daily overall calorie intake is fairly constant from ages two to five. Eating a small amount of food at one meal is usually balanced by eating more at later meals. These findings suggest that children adjust their calorie needs over a twenty-four-hour period.

Young children instinctively eat enough food each day to meet their energy needs and to stay healthy, and they generally don't need adults interfering and trying to force them to eat more of certain foods.

- There are wide differences among children in their ability to regulate energy intake.
- Parents and caregivers who are strict about how they feed a child can negatively affect how the child accepts foods as well as the child's ability to regulate energy intake. Without the ability to naturally regulate caloric intake, children are at risk for weight gain and obesity.
- Young children instinctively eat enough food each day to meet their energy needs and stay healthy; they generally don't need adults interfering and trying to force them to eat more of certain foods.

Four- and five-year-olds enjoy being with other children and adults and they are becoming more verbal, conversational, and social. Mealtimes can now be particularly enjoyable, especially when children sit in small groups and share a meal or snack with one another and/or with adults at their center or school. Mealtimes that are hurried or stressful or that involve threats or punishment interfere with eating and digestion. They slow or even prevent children from developing healthy attitudes toward food and mealtimes.

Safety

The primary causes of injury to four- and five-year-olds are car accidents, falls, burns, choking, poisoning, drowning, and guns. Car accidents rank highest. More children are killed in car accidents, either as passengers or as pedestrians, than by any other hazard.

PLAYGROUND SAFETY

Playgrounds can be designed to encourage creative, positive play and social interaction and to support children's physical and cognitive development. Unfortunately, playground designs have traditionally included equipment that encourages only individual or parallel play and/or equipment that is somewhat dangerous and difficult to keep repaired. Older playgrounds were designed for older children. Playground safety is therefore an important concern for child care staff.

Today's playground designers are trying out materials and designs that are safe and fun, and work for different types of play and different age groups. New playgrounds should have a safe surface underneath all equipment to reduce the chance of injury when children fall. Here are guidelines offered by experts on playground safety:

- Children should always be supervised on playgrounds and encouraged to use the equipment that is best for their age and size. Adults should help children with the equipment as needed.
- Playgrounds and equipment should be regularly inspected and carefully maintained.
- Soft surfaces should be placed underneath playground equipment to reduce the risk of injury from a fall (sand, ten inches deep; wood chips, twelve inches deep; or rubber outdoor mats).
- Guardrails that surround platforms should be at least thirty-eight inches high, and no higher than six feet above the ground.

- There should be no vertical or horizontal spaces between three-and-a-half and nine inches wide (to prevent a small child from getting her head caught).
- Moving parts should be enclosed to prevent children or their clothing from getting caught.
- Construction materials should be chosen with safety in mind: Swing seats, for example, are safer if made of rubber or canvas rather than of wood or metal.
- Equipment should be a safe distance from car and pedestrian traffic areas, and six feet or more from walls or fences.

CHOOSING TOYS, PLAY EQUIPMENT, AND SAFETY GEAR

1. Know the ages, abilities, and interests of the children who will use the equipment.
2. Examine the toy, play equipment, or safety gear thoroughly, and read labels and instructions carefully.
   a. What age child will use the equipment?
   b. Are special skills or information needed to use the item?
   c. Does the item match the child's large- and/or small-motor abilities, cognitive abilities, and interests?
   d. Is it made of nontoxic materials? (Avoid items that carry wording such as "harmful if swallowed," "avoid inhalation," "avoid skin contact," and "use with adequate ventilation.")
   e. Is it motorized, electrical, or battery operated?
   f. Is it manufactured by a trustworthy firm? (Check the Consumer Product Safety Commission reports or child health alerts and other publications for recall and safety histories of toys and play equipment.)
   g. Does the item do what the manufacturer claims it will do?
   h. Is the item sturdy and long-lasting?
3. Examine the item for hazards such as lead-based paint, sharp or protruding points or edges, weak construction, small parts that can be swallowed or cause choking (watch for "eyes," buttons, bells, and other items on dolls and stuffed toys), and flammability.
4. Consider what part of a child's development will be helped with a given piece of equipment.
   a. Physical: large-motor, small-motor, prehension (grasping abilities), pinching movements, and hand–eye, hand–mouth, and eye–foot coordination

b. Cognitive: exploration, curiosity, problem solving, concept formation, connecting ideas or actions, cause-and-effect understanding, associative thinking, and new idea formation

c. Language and literacy: conversation, labels, new concepts, questions, interest in symbols (signs, letters, numerals), vocabulary, and creative use of language through rhymes, storytelling, role playing, songs, and poetry

d. Psychosocial: pure enjoyment, symbolic play, acting, interacting with others, expressing feelings, gaining self-sufficiency and self-confidence, using fantasy and imagination, and gaining positive social understandings

5. Decide whether the item can be used in more than one way and whether it will keep children's interest for a long time.

Burns

Another common injury to young children is burns. The chance of being burned should be less in a child care setting than in a home. Nevertheless, children can be burned in a child care setting by a container of hot food or drink that spills on them; by microwave-heated foods (which often have hot spots) or by heating equipment. All these injuries are preventable. Children generally should not be in a food preparation area unless they are involved in preparation and very closely supervised. Because serious burns can result from hot spots in microwaved foods, doctors advise against microwaving food for infants, toddlers, or young children. If a microwave is used, the food should be stirred, tested for hot spots, and then cooled to a safe temperature before serving. All heating equipment should be put safely behind guards or otherwise separated from areas that children use.

Choking

Choking in young children can be prevented by making careful decisions about what food is served and how it is served. Infants and toddlers are generally at higher risk of choking because they tend to put things in their mouths, because they have immature chewing and swallowing abilities, and because they are easily distracted. Nevertheless, four- and five-year-olds are also liable to choke.

Here is a list of foods and objects most often connected with choking in young children: small items less than a half-inch in diameter; nuts and seeds; spherical or cylinder-shaped foods and objects; buttons, small toys, rocks, grapes, pieces of hot dog, and round hard candies; items of unusual or unfamiliar consistency, such as chewing gum, popcorn, corn, or potato chips; some uncooked vegetables and fruits; sticky foods (peanut butter, caramel candy, dried fruits, raisins); and hard-to-chew meats.

Here are suggestions for lowering the risk of choking:

- Cook food until it is soft enough to be pierced by a fork.
- Substitute thinly sliced meats and well-cooked hamburger for hot dogs.
- Cut food into bite-sized pieces; avoid slippery round shapes.
- Be sure to remove all packaging from foods, such as bits of clinging cellophane or paper.
- Remove bones in chicken, meat, and fish.
- Remove seeds and pits from fruits.
- Avoid the snacks and foods listed in the preceding paragraph.

In addition to carefully selecting and preparing foods, adults *must* watch children at meals and snacktimes. Children should sit when eating. They should be encouraged to eat slowly and to avoid talking and laughing with food in their mouths. All child care professionals should know the American Red Cross first aid procedures for handling a child who is choking.

POISONING

Poisoning is another major safety hazard for young children. Whether swallowed by mouth or absorbed through the skin, hazards exist in many forms: medicines, aerosol sprays, gases, dusts, paints and solvents, commercial dyes, and various art materials (inks, solvent-based glues, chalk dust, tempera paint dust, some crayons, paints, and clay powders). Toxins are also found in building materials (asbestos, formaldehyde, lead-based paint), dishes and ceramics containing lead, tobacco smoke, as well as radon gas in soil.

Preventing childhood poisoning means keeping toxic substances away from children *and* keeping children away from toxins. At child care centers and at home, it's very important to keep medicines, cleaning supplies, and other toxins away from children's reach and stored in *locked* cabinets. The licensing and accreditation standards of child care centers and schools, city ordinances, as well as state and federal regulations must be followed.

WATER SAFETY

Young children and water create another safety concern. Beginning quite early in the toddler period, caregivers must teach children to be careful around water. Infants, toddlers, and preschoolers should never be left unattended in bathtubs, wading pools, or swimming pools or beaches (which demand particular vigilance). Basic water safety instruction for young children includes the following:

- wearing appropriate water safety devices
- using water toys, such as floats, properly
- going into the water only when an adult is present
- keeping breakable toys and dishes away from bodies of water
- walking slowly and carefully on wet surfaces

Adults who care for children must teach, follow, and enforce water safety rules with children. They must know rescue techniques and cardiopulmonary resuscitation (CPR).

Providing swimming lessons for four- and five-year-olds can be a good idea. And yet a child's swimming ability can create a problem when adults become overly confident in the child's abilities. It's very important to remember that even when children are physically mature enough to learn to swim, they lack the mature judgment needed to know when and where to swim,

> *Even when children are physically mature enough to learn to swim, they lack the mature judgment needed to know when and where to swim, or what to do in an emergency.*

or what to do in an emergency. They must still be carefully watched. Remember, it takes only a minute or two for a child to drown.

Types and Quality of Early Care and Education

High-quality child care provides "a nurturing, safe, and stimulating environment for children that promotes their healthy growth and development" (Child Welfare League of America 1997). However, because schools are under state and federal government pressure to improve outcomes, younger and younger children are forced into experiences beyond their capacity. For example, prekindergarten and kindergarten curricula are now more like upper-grade curricula. This often means that young children do not get essential growth-promoting experiences—opportunities for physical and motor activity, for example—that we now know are essential for their neurological development and overall health and well-being.

Some child development experts are concerned about the effect that spending so much time away from the care of parents will have on children. They worry that children's psychosocial and physical/motor development will be diminished because of the stress and fatigue associated with long days; multiple settings; different adult personalities and expectations; changing groups of children; and varying standards and rules for protecting health and safety. Child care providers can help reduce children's stress and fatigue by doing the following:

- providing regularly scheduled and nutritious meals and snacks, lots of fresh drinking water, and easy access to toilet facilities
- providing regularly scheduled rest periods and naptimes, as well as rest periods as needed
- hiring teachers and staff who have knowledge and training in child development, and who understand how multiple settings, numerous caregivers, and long days affect children
- having regular outdoor playtimes for children to provide stress-relieving fresh air, sunshine, exercise, and spontaneous play
- allowing children to make as many choices throughout the day as is reasonable and possible—choices about learning centers, materials and activities, playmates, snacks, and so on
- providing opportunities and safe spaces to play alone without pressure to interact with others
- allowing children to participate in classroom and group rule-making to decrease the stress of dealing with too many rules and standards
- carefully watching the general health of individual children and giving quick attention to signs of stress, fatigue, and/or impending illness

Because there are so many school and child care programs, it's very important that all programs and services for children and their families communicate and work together. The length of the school day and the length of the school year in public schools demand a concerted effort to create links among Head Start programs, child care providers, public schools, health and social services, and families.

Reference
Child Welfare League of America. 1997. *Guarding children's rights—Serving children's needs*. New York: Child Welfare League of America.

The Role of the Early Childhood Professional

1. Provide safe and healthy surroundings for children.
2. Provide for children's nutritional needs.
3. Keep track of children's immunizations and other protections from disease.
4. Encourage regular dental examinations.
5. Establish healthy routines for rest, sleep, play, and activity.
6. Reduce the stress-producing events in children's lives.
7. Support children's growing large- and small-motor abilities and body awareness.
8. Provide age-appropriate and developmentally appropriate toys, equipment, and material.
9. Ensure children's safety by having adequate supervision; by monitoring the types and condition of toys, materials, and equipment; and by removing environmental hazards.
10. Provide opportunities for satisfying and supportive psychosocial interactions between children and their parents, other adults, and other children.
11. Help children increase their awareness of health and safety practices.
12. Encourage children to begin taking responsibility for maintaining their own health and safety.

Discussion Questions

1. On pages 7–8, review the list of large-motor skills deemed important for four- and five-year-olds to acquire. What are some games that might help children develop these skills? For example, hopscotch is a game that children like to play that also helps them strengthen their hopping skills.
2. What types of sensory experiences do you have available for the preschoolers in your setting? Make a list of potential field trips appropriate for preschoolers where they could engage all their senses; for example, a trip to an apple orchard or a children's museum. If you're not able to take the children on such a field trip, could you replicate the experience in your setting? How might you replicate an apple orchard experience, for example?
3. How do you introduce the concepts of similarity and difference to the preschoolers in your program? If your program is not culturally diverse, how might you begin to teach preschoolers to respect others who look or talk differently than they do? If your program is culturally diverse, how do you show respect for the differing beliefs and practices of the families in your program? Make a plan for addressing these issues.
4. Based on the safety suggestions offered in this chapter, perform a safety

check of your facility (or home if you're a family care provider) and outdoor play area, or invite an experienced professional to come and do a check for you. Are there improvements you could make? If so, develop a timeline to address them.

Further Reading

Aronson, S. 2003. *Healthy young children: A manual for programs.* 4th ed. Washington, D.C.: National Association for the Education of Young Children.

Brown, W. H., M. A. Conroy. 1997. *Including and supporting preschool children with developmental delays in early childhood programs.* Little Rock, Ark.: Southern Early Childhood Association.

Greenman, J. 1999. *Places for childhoods: Making quality happen in the real world.* Redman, Wash.: Child Care Information Exchange.

Kostelnik, M. J., E. Onaga, B. Rhode, and A. Whiren. 2002. *Children with special needs.* New York: Teachers College Press.

McCraken, J. B. 1999. *Playgrounds: Safe and sound.* Washington, D.C.: National Association for the Education of Young Children.

Perry, J. P. 2001. *Outdoor play: Teaching strategies with young children.* New York: Teachers College Press.

Sanders, S. W. 2002. *Active for life: Developmentally appropriate movement programs for young children.* Washington, D.C.: National Association for the Education of Young Children.

Other Resources

- American Academy of Pediatrics
  141 Northwest Point Boulevard
  P.O. Box 927
  Elk Grove Village, IL 60007
  847-434-4000
  www.aap.org

- American Academy of Pediatrics
  Brochures (guidelines for parents) on numerous topics are available through local pediatricians' offices. Some example titles are as follows:
  Ear infections and children
  Your child's eyes
  Anemia and your young child
  Choking prevention and first aid for infants and children
  Common childhood infections
  Your child and the environment

Know the facts about HIV and AIDS
Allergies in children: Guidelines for parents

- American Academy of Pediatrics
  Healthy Child Care America
  www.healthychildcare.org

- Americans with Disabilities Act Accessibility Guidelines for Play Areas
  www.access-board.gov/play/Finalrule.htm

- Center for Early Education and Development (CEED)
  University of Minnesota
  215 Pattee Hall
  150 Pillsbury Drive SE
  Minneapolis, MN 55455
  612-624-5780
  www.education.umn.edu/CEED/

- For more information on the effects of TV watching on social and emotional behavior, creativity, language skills, and school achievement, go to http://www.kidsource.com/kidsource/content/TV.viewing.html.

- National Institute of Child Health and Human Development
  http://www.nichd.nih.gov/default.htm

- National Resource Center for Health and Safety in Child Care and Early Education
  http://nrc.uchsc.edu

- Fireproof Children/Prevention First
  www.playsafe@fireproofchildren.com

- Play Safe! Be Safe!
  www.playsafebesafe.com

Part Two

Psychosocial Development

And the first step, as you know, is always what matters most, particularly when we are dealing with those who are young and tender. That is the time when they are taking shape and when any impression we choose to make leaves a permanent mark.

—PLATO

In contrast to toddlers, four- and five-year-olds are calm and poised. As their motor abilities improve, they can do more for themselves and be more independent. As their cognitive abilities continue to develop, they form clearer perceptions and can understand more. Rapid growth in language skills helps them better communicate with friends and caregivers. Greater patience in getting their wants and needs met improves their interactions with others. They enjoy being with and playing with other kids their age, and as a result, their social group expands beyond their parents and other caregivers. During play they are more focused and cooperative. Thus preschoolers are friendlier, more sociable, controllable, and predictable.

Part 2 looks at psychosocial development. By the time children are four or five years old, their broad range of experiences—including positive and negative attachments—has influenced their development. Here, you'll explore the effects of early experiences in later life and explore whether the effects of negative experiences can be overcome. Children are now beginning to understand social situations, so you'll also learn about the three forms of social understanding; children's moral development at this age; and the ways child care professionals can encourage social and moral development. Learning how four- and five-year-olds name, understand, control, and express their many emotions—a huge developmental challenge—is also covered here. You'll learn how children's sense of self grows as they become aware of individual differences in physical characteristics, gender, and abilities. Finally, part 2 will describe studies of child-rearing practices that can give you much insight into the kind of adult–child interactions that help children learn cooperation and self-control.

4 Theories of Psychosocial Development

For centuries, philosophers and psychologists have believed that events in the earliest years of a child's life influence later development, often in critical ways. Similarly, most child development theorists place great importance on the type and quality of experiences in children's first three to four years. Today, philosophers, theorists, and scientists continue to study the relationship between the experiences of infancy and childhood and later development and behavior.

Erik Erikson's Stages of Development

Erik Erikson's theory of psychosocial development, with its series of recognizable stages, supports the idea that early experiences influence later development. Erikson's work, which examined the emotional and social interactions between children and their caregivers, is important for parents and child care professionals. It shows how children build a foundation for emotional and social development and mental health. His eight stages describe developmental changes from infancy through adulthood. He believed there is a task each of us must complete at each stage of development. How we complete a given stage, or fail to do so, affects the next stage. As we pass through each stage, we develop personality strengths (or weaknesses) based on what we accomplish during that stage. In addition, we experience conflicts, especially during our adolescent years, as we progress toward adulthood. It was Erikson who invented the term *identity crisis*. He believed that while certain tasks ideally needed to be completed during each stage, it is still possible for people later in life to work on tasks they did not successfully complete earlier in life. (For more on Erikson's theories, see part 2 of *Understanding Infant Development*.)

Today, many child development experts believe that successful outcomes at each of Erikson's eight stages of personality development prepare children for the ensuing stages. It is in the eighth stage that the adult personality achieves what Erikson called *ego integrity*. Adults with ego integrity are able to follow the rules of their culture and to accept the responsibility of leadership. Adults who care for children work to give them the essential experiences they need to develop a well-integrated personality.

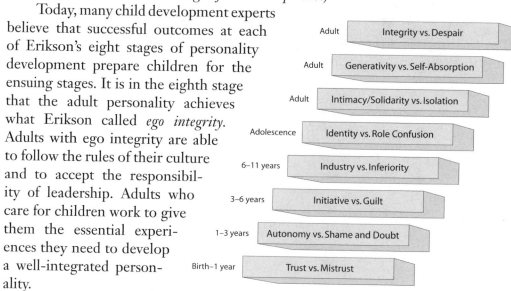

Adult — Integrity vs. Despair
Adult — Generativity vs. Self-Absorption
Adult — Intimacy/Solidarity vs. Isolation
Adolescence — Identity vs. Role Confusion
6–11 years — Industry vs. Inferiority
3–6 years — Initiative vs. Guilt
1–3 years — Autonomy vs. Shame and Doubt
Birth–1 year — Trust vs. Mistrust

Effects of Poor or Interrupted Early Attachments

Many child development researchers have looked at the effects of early attachment problems on later psychosocial development. Physical or psychological illness, marriage problems, divorce, multiple foster care assignments, reversing of adoption decisions, and a number of other problems can cause the relationship between a child and his attachment person to break. When this happens, it's not unusual for the child to experience attachment problems that interfere with psychosocial development.

Researchers have found that interrupted or broken attachments can cause the following behaviors in young children, as outlined by Charles Zeanah, O. K. Mammen, and Alicia Lieberman (1993):

- Unusual and/or extreme expressions of affection. Such children may have no warm or affectionate interactions with potential attachment persons and/or they may become affectionate with everyone they meet, including total strangers.
- Unusual comfort-seeking behaviors when hurt, frightened, or ill. For example, failing to ask for help from a trusted attachment person or being overly careful when doing this.
- Becoming extremely dependent on adults or being unable to ask for and use adult support even when needed.

- Refusing to follow rules or being very worried about an inability to follow every part of any rule or suggestion.
- Failing to look for a caregiver and/or support in unfamiliar situations.
- Responding to caregivers by trying to control them, by being mean to them or by being unusually kind to them.
- Acting very detached when reuniting with a caregiver after being separated for a time; avoiding others; having angry outbursts; or not showing affection.

Studies of securely attached infants show they're more comfortable socially when they start preschool and they're more responsive to their peers in kindergarten. They also tend to be less dependent on adults and more curious than children who don't have secure attachments; are better able to handle stress; and are better at problem-solving and memory tasks in preschool. Many studies of early attachment successes and failures support the theories that early attachment experiences *do* have important long-term effects on psychosocial development.

SECURE ATTACHMENTS CAN COMPENSATE FOR EARLY PROBLEMS

While broken attachments cause children psychological harm, the situation is not hopeless. Over time, the results of secure and insecure attachments alike are affected by other factors. For example, children who are insecurely attached to one parent may find security and support through a strong attachment to the other parent, to a relative, or to some other important adult in their lives. That's why in nonparental caregiving settings such as child care centers, stable, predictable, supportive relationships with caregivers who are emotionally available are crucial. In the end, the long-term consequences depend on the length of time the child experiences a particular kind of attachment and the nurturing ability of the caregiver.

Secure attachments during the infant and toddler periods make the transition into later attachment stages smoother and easier. Around age three, children begin having what are called *partnership behaviors*. During this stage, children are better able to understand others' intentions and can adapt their behavior and work more cooperatively with others. Parent–child interactions can be more goal oriented as well. While four- and five-year-olds still rely on parents for security and comfort, they are beginning to focus more attention on their own friends and will more often rely on friends for social and emotional support.

While it's very important to pay attention to the quality of infant and early childhood experiences, it helps to understand that growth and development continue throughout life. We learn from and build on our experiences as the years pass, and from birth to death our individual development is affected, both positively and negatively, by our biology, our ability to adapt, and our experiences. Our overall level of health affects growth and development, of course, but there are other factors: personality and behavior, social/cultural rules, parenting and discipline techniques, family expectations and patterns of interaction, unusual or stressful events, individual or family joy, success, disappointment, traumatic experiences, and role models.

Child development experts usually emphasize on the early formative months and years, but it's important to remember that in most cases, single events in early childhood do not cause behaviors that can't be changed by new experiences and/or by strength and ability to adapt over the years. While certain early experiences are considered essential for the best possible development, it's our experiences over many years that have a long-term effect on development. Nevertheless, experts still believe that when healthy growth and development are at risk, it's very important to intervene as soon as possible with medical, social, and educational help.

Psychosocial Theory: Initiative versus Guilt

The four- to five-year-old has entered Erikson's third stage of psychosocial development, as shown in figure 4.1 on page 38. Building on the previous stages of trust and autonomy, four- and five-year-olds are now struggling between a sense of *initiative* and a sense of guilt.

FOSTERING INITIATIVE

Children at this age have a growing sense of initiative. They *want* to master new skills and use language to ask questions. Their social circle is expanding rapidly and they very much want to play with others. Their improved motor skills allow them to try new activities, such as climbing on playground equipment or riding a bicycle without training wheels. They are eager to learn and truly enjoy the activities that help them better understand their constantly expanding world. This is a time when planning and anticipating coming activities and doing things with others are particularly enjoyable. Helping to plan a family outing or helping to prepare the classroom for a special visitor are exciting and give children a new sense of purpose.

Four- and five-year-olds' play is more social and complicated than toddlers' play. Imitation, imagination, and fantasy lead to complex and ever-changing "plays" that grow and change with new fantasies, plots, and characters as different children enter and leave the playgroup.

This developing sense of initiative isn't always used in a positive way. Children can become both physically and verbally aggressive. Pushing a playmate aside to be next on the balance beam or threatening another child are examples of using force as a way to control others. Threats such as "I won't be your best friend" or "You can't come to my birthday party" are examples of inappropriate initiative. As their verbal skills grow, children this age also sometimes use words to shock and deceive others.

> *Children this age have a growing sense of initiative. In other words, they want to master new skills, use language to ask questions, and include others in their work and play.*

AVOIDING GUILT

Inappropriate initiative can cause children this age to feel anxious, embarrassed, and guilty when they realize their behaviors aren't acceptable to others or have hurt others. Children often are unsure how to act, so it's important for the adults in their lives to suggest better behaviors and guide them toward positive, more constructive outcomes. Such guidance, however, must provide a balance between control and freedom for the child. Too little guidance (undercontrolling) or too much guidance (overcontrolling) won't teach alternative behavior. Instead, these responses can weaken children's opportunities to learn appropriate behaviors.

Overcontrolling and undercontrolling can also contribute to a child's sense of guilt. When their efforts to express feelings and interests or to initiate ideas and activities are stopped, children can develop a lack of self-confidence that will continue as they get older. Responses that can stop children's growing sense of initiative and self-confidence include power-assertive discipline techniques; too much criticism or too many corrections or warnings; teasing or ridiculing; or belittling their questions or their pretend play. These kinds of interactions can hurt children and should be avoided.

When children's sense of guilt is greater than their sense of initiative, they tend to look for too much assurance and permission from adults and peers. They are more vulnerable to the suggestions of others and may tend to follow others without thinking about what they're doing, sometimes following poor role models. They're often targeted by bullies. They hesitate to take risks, try new activities, reach out to others for interactions, or say what they want. As a result, they can't completely enjoy their new abilities.

Egocentric Behavior

Few preschool teachers and child care providers would disagree that four- and five-year-old children exhibit *egocentric behavior.* This means that preschoolers believe that others are experiencing the world in the same manner they are. Through social interactions in preschools and child care settings, young children begin to realize that other children have needs and wishes, too, and that those desires can be different from their own.

Because preschoolers are so focused on their own perspectives, a group of fifteen four- or five-year-olds can present fifteen or more competing requests for a teacher's attention. Here are a few examples:

- In the middle of a fingerplay, Justin discovers a hangnail on one of his fingers, leaves his seated position, and climbs over the group to show his injured finger to the teacher.
- On arrival at kindergarten, Beth asks her teacher, "Do you want to see what I brought in my lunch today?"
- During the school nurse's demonstration of hand washing, Kari says, "You know what? My daddy washed his new car last night."
- Deon shouts from across the room, "Teacher, Shannon is sitting in my chair!"

Social Understanding

By the time children are four or five years old, they've already spent quite a bit of time watching other children and adults, and they've met and interacted with many different people. Social cognitive theory places a great deal of importance on the influence of role models.

Preschoolers are beginning to understand social situations. You can see this in their ability to make social judgments on the basis of past experience, in their observations of other people, and in their viewpoints and expectations of others. This social understanding is characterized in part by a growing awareness of the effects of their behaviors on others and by their increasing (though still not perfect) ability to understand others' viewpoints. They may, for example, be able to control some of their aggressive behavior because they still remember how some aggressive action hurt a friend. Through experience (and perhaps with help from adults), children can also learn that being kind to others brings out warm and friendly responses from them.

Child development researchers Rubin and Everett (1982) have identified three forms of social understanding:

1. Cognitive perspective-taking, which includes the ability to consider others' thoughts and intentions
2. Emotional perspective-taking, or the ability to notice and think about the feelings and emotions of others
3. Spatial perspective-taking, or the ability to consider another person's physical view of the world

A child who pretends to be a veterinarian, for example, may be showing cognitive perspective-taking. A child who attempts to comfort a crying playmate may be showing emotional perspective-taking, which is an awareness of the other child's problem or its cause. A child who removes an obstacle from the path of another, thus preventing an accident, is demonstrating spatial perspective-taking.

Adults can help children develop perspective-taking abilities by helping them to think about the feelings and experiences of others in real-life situations.

Children at this age love to make up "plays" in which ideas and plots come from real-life experiences. The pretending that takes place in this kind of play helps children better understand the perspectives of others. As children act out different roles, such as "You be the nurse and I'll be sick," they become aware of the roles people in their culture have. As they act out a given scene, they discover differences between what they want and what their playmates want. By changing their play to meet the wishes of the other children involved, they are developing an ability to understand other perspectives.

Children can also learn about other perspectives through books. The conversations in children's stories can be used to show four- and five-year-olds the feelings and experiences of the characters. Adults can help them compare their own experiences and feelings to those of the characters in stories. Adults can also help children develop perspective-taking abilities by helping them to think about the feelings and experiences of others in real-life situations. In the course of a day, you'll find there are many opportunities to help young children develop perspective-taking abilities. For example:

- "How do you think Tony felt when you knocked over his block tower? Let's let Tony tell us what he thinks about what happened."
- "Did you notice how Ms. Jones smiled when you helped open the door for her?"
- "Did you notice how your baby sister stopped crying and listened when you were singing to her?"

- "What kinds of things make us happy? . . . angry? . . . sad?"
- "If you stand over here, you can see what LaToya is describing."
- "You helped prevent an accident by moving that tricycle out of the pathway."

Prosocial Development

Four- and five-year-olds are beginning to develop what are called *prosocial* behaviors (positive social behaviors). These behaviors include *empathy* and *altruism*.

> Definition: *Empathy*—the ability to recognize the feelings of others, such as suffering, worry, or happiness, and to be able to imagine what those feelings are like.

> Definition: *Altruism*—behavior that is intended to help another without expecting any reward.

In young children, a number of factors influence prosocial behaviors, including age, cognitive level, perspective-taking ability, individual personality, family interactions, and role models. Studies show that when children see prosocial behaviors in adults, they generally become more prosocial themselves. This is particularly true when the child and the adult have a warm relationship and the child has been nurtured by that adult.

> *Angela's friend Mia has just recovered from a lung infection and is finally able to see friends again. Cheryl says hello to Mia and then sends the two children off to play. Angela is clearly happy to see her friend again, but she's concerned about the way her mom greeted Mia.*
>
> *Angela and Mia become involved in a new and rather difficult puzzle. Needing help, Angela runs to get her mom. As they walk back to where the puzzle is set up, Angela says, "You didn't tell Mia you were sorry." Confused, her mother asks, "About what, Angela?" "About she's been sick," replies Angela.*

Why was Angela concerned? When she's been sick, she's heard her mom use such expressions as "I'm so sorry you're not feeling well" and "I'm really glad you feel better today." She's also heard her mom express such feelings to others. By watching her parents and other adults, Angela learned to express concern for others, and she noticed when her mother said nothing to Mia. Studies of parenting styles, guidance techniques, and the effect of role models shows that when young children see examples of prosocial behavior, they're more likely to model that behavior in other situations.

In addition to role modeling and guidance techniques, caregivers can encourage prosocial development in the following ways:

1. Provide experiences that promote self-esteem, because research shows that good feelings about oneself are related to more cooperative behaviors in four- and five-year-olds.
2. Give age-appropriate responsibilities. With such experiences, children come to feel they are a contributing part of the family, class, or group.
3. Create opportunities for four- and five-year-olds to interact with other children and to participate in pretend play. Such experiences promote role playing and the ability to see others' perspectives.
4. Create opportunities for children to participate in noncompetitive, cooperative games and group activities.
5. Expose children to literature, television programs, toys, and computer and video games that support prosocial themes.

Moral Development

The most famous theory of cognitive development is that of Jean Piaget, who was born in 1896 in Switzerland. His research had one primary goal: to understand how human knowledge grows, especially in children. Piaget's studies of cognitive development have dominated the fields of child studies, psychology, philosophy, and education since the 1920s. Even though other theorists have questioned or modified Piaget's theory, his ideas still greatly affect early childhood education.

Young children think and solve problems quite differently than older children and adults.

One of Piaget's most important ideas was that young children think and solve problems quite differently than older children and adults. As caregivers, it's important to understand these differences so that you can respond to and interact with young children in ways that will most help their cognitive development.

FOUR STAGES OF COGNITIVE DEVELOPMENT

Piaget's theory defines four major stages of cognitive development: the *sensorimotor period* (birth to age two), the *preoperational period* (ages two to seven), the *concrete operations period* (ages seven to eleven), and the *formal operations period* (age eleven and beyond).

His studies of moral development focus on how children develop a respect for rules and a sense of justice. He proposes a sequence of moral development consisting of a *premoral* stage, a stage of *moral realism,* and a stage of *moral relativism.* While these theories can help you as a child care professional better understand the behavior of the children in your care and support their moral development, the names of these stages are not as important as understanding the process.

> Definition: *Premoral stage*—Piaget's earliest stage of moral development where children prior to age six have little or no concern for rules and don't understand how or why we use them.

Child development experts, like Piaget, believe that children under age six are in a *premoral* stage of morality because they have little or no concern for rules. For instance, children in playgroups often make up rules as they play and change them whenever they want. They have little idea of how or why we use rules.

Toward the end of the premoral stage, children begin to show signs of Piaget's second stage, *moral realism.* During this stage, they are very strict about rules and think they can't and shouldn't be changed because they're made by all-knowing authority figures (God, parents, teachers). They believe that whether a person's behavior is "right" or "wrong" depends on whether they've followed the rules. Because they're so egocentric, children at this age believe everyone should follow the same rules and understand them in the same way.

> Definition: *Moral realism*—a sense of morals that focuses on rules and consequences rather than on the intentions behind an action.

At this stage of morality, children think about punishment as it relates to breaking a rule, usually without considering the rule breaker's intentions. For young moralists, punishment should happen quickly when rules are broken. Some children at this stage may believe that injury or bad luck after some misdeed is deserved: a rule has been broken. If they can't make their playmates follow rules, older preschoolers will sometimes get help by telling an adult. This behavior is a natural part of the child's growing sense of rules and not necessarily an attempt to be unkind to a playmate. Later, children begin to move into the stage of *moral relativism* and begin considering the intentions of the person breaking the rule.

Definition: *Moral relativism*—at this stage of morality, children begin to consider the intentions of the person breaking the rule.

Kohlberg's Developmental Sequence of Moral Thinking

Lawrence Kohlberg expanded on Piaget's theory, creating three levels of moral thinking similar to Piaget's: *preconventional* (premoral), *conventional*, and *postconventional*. He believes children pass through each stage at a unique rate.

PRECONVENTIONAL LEVEL

Stage 1: Children's moral behaviors are focused on punishment, and children rarely, if ever, question people in power, such as teachers or parents. To them, an action's "goodness" or "badness" completely depends on its physical consequences.

Stage 2: Children believe that "right" actions are those that satisfy their needs (and occasionally the needs of others). They will consider the ideas of fairness and sharing, but only if of benefit to themselves. A good example of this type of thinking is "You help me and I'll help you."

CONVENTIONAL LEVEL

Stage 3: Children have a "good boy/good girl" point of view. To children in this stage, "good" behavior pleases or helps others. They strongly believe that what "most people do" is the right thing to do. They try to get others' approval by being "nice."

Stage 4: Children's behaviors are focused on authority, rules, and keeping social order. "Right" behavior means doing one's duty, showing respect for authority, and maintaining the social order for its own sake.

POSTCONVENTIONAL LEVEL

At this stage, children begin to understand that there are certain moral principles that apply to people but that are independent of the people or groups in authority. As with Piaget's moral relativism stage, children don't begin to move into the postconventional stage until they are older.

Chapter 5 looks at how brain development helps preschoolers identify and control their emotional responses as they learn self-control and compliance.

References

Rubin, K. H., and B. Everett. 1982. Social perspective-taking in young children. In *The young child: Reviews of research*, vol. 3., ed S. G. Moore and C. R. Cooper, 97–113. Washington, D.C.: National Association for the Education of Young Children.

Zeanah, C. H., Jr., O. K. Mammen, and A. E. Lieberman. 1993. Disorders of attachment. In *Handbook of infant mental health*, ed. C. H. Zeanah Jr., 332–349. New York: Guilford Press.

5 Dimensions of Psychosocial Development

As young children continue to grow and mature, their brain chemistry and neurological wiring become more active in order to regulate their emotional responses to new experiences.

Neurological Development

Far more neural fibers spring from the brain's emotional center than from the larger rational thinking centers. This is why emotions can so strongly affect preschoolers' behavior, often dominating intelligent or rational thought. For example, the need to share and take turns may be a rational concept that four- and five-year-olds can intellectually understand. However, their emotion-driven desire to have and enjoy a particular toy often overcomes this understanding. It takes some time before their understanding can overcome their emotional desire to have the toy. We know that four- and five-year-olds' inability to delay getting what they want, to use reason rather than emotion, and to use self-control are partly the result of incomplete brain wiring and chemistry.

When an emotional reaction is particularly strong, the nervous system goes into what is called a "fight-or-flight" stress mode. This response can be both lifesaving and problematic. On the one hand, it tells us that we may be in some kind of danger and helps us react quickly. On the other hand, past experiences (abuse, neglect, and other stressful events) can cause changes in the brain that make us react to a situation before we can think about what is happening. Road rage in adults is a serious and frightening example of the power of emotion over reason. Fortunately, most people develop the ability to think before acting.

As scientific research continues to show that neglect and abuse harm the developing brain, we recognize how important it is for parents and child care professionals to provide essential psychological nourishment with warm, affectionate, and helpful interactions.

Emotional Development

Like adults, young children experience a range of emotions, from joy and delight to sadness and despair. Children express feelings of love, acceptance, frustration, anger, hostility, jealousy, shame, embarrassment, guilt, anxiety, fear, distress, depression, pride, humor, surprise, and more. They express these emotions in many ways: by crying, shouting, pouting, being alone, being inattentive, being silly, talking about emotional events or feelings, and by rejecting others and their efforts to console, and so on. Learning to better understand, control, and express emotions is one of the key psychosocial goals for preschoolers. To do this, they need to be able to do the following:

- understand the idea of emotions
- think about the types of situations that cause certain emotional reactions for them
- understand how their expressions of emotions affect others

An important first step in a young child's understanding of emotions is labeling them. Labeling emotions happens when caregivers tell children the names for emotions and identify emotional events. For example, a caregiver might say:

- "You are really *angry*."
- "Do you feel *unhappy* when your dad and mom are away at work?"
- "It makes all of us *sad* when someone dies."
- "When you feel *mad* at someone, let's talk about it."
- "I can tell you're very *proud* of yourself."
- "We're all having such a *happy* time today."

Names can only help so much, however. *Talking* with children about feelings is also very important. For example, you might talk with children about the following:

- the kinds of situations that bring out certain behaviors
- how different people respond in different situations
- appropriate and inappropriate, effective and ineffective, healthy and unhealthy ways to express and deal with feelings
- how the way we express emotions affects others

Helping children name and manage emotions is essential to their overall mental health and their social development, including their ability to relate to and understand others' feelings. By the time children are four or five years old, they have some understanding of their own emotions and the emotions of others. They have the capacity to think about their feelings and understand that feelings stay for a while after the event that caused them. At this point, however, emotional control is a long way off. During this stage, children are beginning to learn and apply rules, to show that they know a little about when and where certain expressions of emotion are acceptable. They are beginning to control how they express their emotions in ways that help them, and they are becoming aware of the effects that their expression of emotion has on others.

> *Helping children name and manage emotions is essential to their overall mental health and their social development, including their ability to relate to and understand others' feelings.*

FEAR AND ANXIETY

All children experience fear and anxiety from time to time. However, not all children have the same fears. For example, some fear the dark, while others do not. Children respond to fear differently, too. One child quietly withdraws or stands near a trusted adult; another cries loudly and holds on tightly. Still others run from a scary situation.

A common source of four- and five-year-olds' fear is this: they don't have enough experience, information, or understanding of the world. For example, after her parents' divorce, Josie became afraid of her own desires and actions because she was worried that somehow she'd "make" her other parent leave her. Other fears arise because children aren't able to separate fantasy and reality. ("Get the bogeyman out of my closet!") Children may also learn to be afraid by watching and imitating their parents, siblings, relatives, or friends. For example, Franky's mother was very afraid of heights, and as a result of her many comments, he began to fear high places too. Fears are also learned through one's own experience; a child who is bitten by a dog becomes afraid of all dogs—a fear that may continue into adulthood. Of course, many fears or anxieties serve an important purpose. It's healthy and wise to be afraid of traffic, strange animals, motorized tools and equipment, fires, and guns because they can be dangerous.

Some children do not develop a healthy fear of danger. They need help from adults to protect them from situations they *should* be afraid of. This guidance should give accurate information without instilling curiosity, which can lead them into dangerous situations. For example, telling a child that "The gun is locked away because guns are very dangerous and can injure and kill" is better than "Don't you dare touch that gun," which, for some children, virtually guarantees they will try to experiment with the forbidden item.

You can help young children understand and cope with fears by giving them appropriate experiences, explanations, and encouragement using appropriate language. When adults are calm, encouraging, and wise, children feel comforted. In time, some fears disappear, although new fears may emerge.

ANGER AND AGGRESSION

Young children can become angry when they don't get what they need or want—such as a person's attention—or when a toy doesn't work or a playmate doesn't respond in an expected way. Confusing discipline or rules they don't like can also bring out anger in children. They get angry when they are hit, pushed, or teased, or when they feel rejected. How quickly a child gets angry, and over what issues, differs from child to child based on differences in temperament, cognitive ability, family and cultural expectations, and role models.

Aggression is behavior that is directed at another person, animal, or object with the intention to threaten or harm. Children can become aggressive when something prevents them from getting what they want. Usually young children are not *intentionally* hurtful or harsh. Injuries or insults tend to be accidental and are due to a child's immaturity. They can be caused by poor motor control (accidentally running into another block construction, knocking it over); poor perspective-taking ability that can result in blunt or insensitive comments ("Why is your hair ugly today?"); or simple misunderstanding (taking over a play space or play item they thought was no longer wanted). Hostile or bullying aggression, on the other hand, intends to threaten, stop, or hurt and is generally unprovoked.

It's important to understand that how you respond to aggressive behavior can affect whether and how often it will happen again. For instance, when an aggressive child succeeds in hurting, intimidating, or causing another child to back away, this "victory" increases the chance he will attempt aggressive behavior again. When adults do not get involved after an incident, children may think the behavior is acceptable—again, increasing the chance the behavior will be repeated. What's more, parents or teachers may even reinforce aggressive attitudes and behaviors. They do this by directly or indirectly encouraging aggression by praising children who use it to get what they want, coaching them to use it, urging children to "stand up for themselves," or by laughing at, teasing, or shaming the child who has been the victim.

As with other social skills, children learn aggressive behaviors from a variety of role models. Parents and teachers teach children to be more aggressive by using disciplinary techniques that are power-assertive, punishing, and/or cause physical pain. Researchers have found that children who have been severely punished don't learn how to think about the reason for others' behaviors. Instead, they simply react more quickly to other children's accidental aggressions—thinking they are intentional or hostile and thus deserve an aggressive response. These scholars believe that severely punished children develop ongoing patterns of misunderstanding others' actions. Such children think any unpleasant interaction with others is hostile and directed at them. If such a pattern continues, children get stuck in a cycle in which their hostile actions cause hostility in others, which in turn confirms their mistaken ideas about themselves and the intentions of others toward them. The result is ongoing aggression.

It's important to understand that caregivers can take action to reduce or eliminate the causes of anger and aggression in young children. Problem areas include:

- family life patterns
- sibling relationships
- discipline techniques
- stress
- physical issues (hunger, fatigue, illness, effects of medications)
- role models
- playmates
- toy preferences
- media influences

Understanding which of these problem areas is contributing to a child's anger and aggression is an important first step.

As a child care professional, you play an important role in helping children understand how to manage anger. First, you can teach them the importance of seeking adult help to resolve conflicts; techniques for resolving conflicts without adult help; ways to accept and talk about anger and what makes them and others angry; rules for showing anger; and constructive ways to manage anger. It's important to accept anger in children; it's normal. Second, you can be their role model by showing them the healthy ways you handle your own anger (instead of simply yelling or blaming).

SELF-COMFORTING BEHAVIORS

At ages four and five, children may still use old self-comforting strategies from time to time to help them cope with uncomfortable or disturbing emotional events. For example, they may use thumb-sucking, retreat to an especially safe or comfortable place, curl up in a favorite blanket, cuddle a stuffed animal, or snuggle up to a trusted playmate or caregiver. All these strategies help children handle their emotions. Learning to recognize and accept one's emotions and to handle them in healthy, positive ways—developing what is called *emotional intelligence*—is an essential part of the socialization process. It promotes good mental health and helps children develop satisfying relationships as they grow older and become adults.

Definition: *Emotional intelligence*—having the ability to recognize and accept one's emotions and to handle them in healthy ways.

Transitional Objects

Although the importance of *transitional objects*—items used for self-comforting, such as favorite blankets or stuffed toys—differs from child to child, such objects remain an important part of the psychosocial development of four- and five-year-olds. Some children stay attached to an object for years, while for others the attachments may be short and change from one object to another. Affection for these special objects can be very strong. Some children talk about how they "love" them.

Some children carry their special object in the car on the way to school, but then leave it in the car during school, awaiting reunion when the school day is over. Others carry the special object into the classroom, but then put it in a cubby, where they can visit it when they want during the day. The need for transitional objects decreases as children move their energy and attention from themselves to others, and from fantasy to real-life tasks.

However, children themselves must make the decision to give up their transitional object. Using force, teasing, making hurtful comments, or otherwise attempting to separate the child from the object only increases the desire to keep it.

Jeremy's parents and teachers are encouraging his interest in dinosaurs by giving him books on the subject. Each morning, his parents get his backpack ready for school with one or two of his favorite dinosaur books and his well-worn teddy bear. Throughout his kindergarten year, Jeremy carries his teddy bear to school with him, carefully tucked in his backpack.

While Jeremy's cognitive abilities are advanced for his age, he still needs a transitional object to comfort himself throughout the day. Sometimes a child's maturity in other areas leads adults to believe that the need for the object should have been outgrown. But this is not always true.

Self-Concept and Self-Esteem

During infancy and toddlerhood, children become more and more self-aware. With a growing sense of independence, four- and five-year-olds begin to describe themselves according to skills they've mastered. Their self-concept is based mostly on a new awareness of their physical qualities and abilities, and on their possessions. They make statements such as "I'm bigger," "I can tie my shoes," and "Watch me skip." They may also describe themselves in relation to their age or to the things they own; for example, they may say, "I'm going to be four on my birthday" or "I have a new bicycle with training wheels." A positive self-concept promotes self-confidence and the belief that mastering life's challenges is possible. It will be a while, however, before a child's self-definition includes inner qualities or character traits.

Children develop positive self-concepts and self-esteem from their experiences with people who are important to them: their parents, siblings, other family members, caregivers, and teachers. Over time, they build an image of themselves that matches other people's attitudes about them. When responses are respectful and encouraging, a child's self-concept will be self-affirming. And when parents and teachers use positive forms of discipline and guidance, a child develops a more balanced self-concept, thinks more positively about herself, and has a higher level of self-esteem than a child who has not experienced such positive interactions. Relationships that provide unconditional love and acceptance, genuine interest and concern, and positive guidance should not, however, be confused with permissive discipline that fails to communicate expected behaviors and value systems. Adults communicate unconditional acceptance when they honor children's feelings and perspectives, and support their competence and worth, while placing limits on inappropriate behaviors. However, when a child's interactions with important adults are humiliating, detached, or unsupportive, that child builds a self-concept that is distorted.

You can gauge the level of children's self-esteem by observing their social interactions. For example, children with low self-esteem are more likely to display shy, aggressive, or antisocial behavior. Their caregivers may, in turn, respond to this behavior less favorably than they do other children. Thus, the negative self-concept is reinforced, and the behaviors repeat themselves in future interactions with adults and children alike. It is possible, though difficult, to break a negative cycle. To do so requires sensitive and helpful responses from adults to support and reinforce a child's worth and competence while coaching and reinforcing more positive interactions with others.

Children can have difficulty forming positive self-concepts and developing self-esteem for many reasons, including parenting and child care practices that block this development. Other factors include developmentally inappropriate expectations; limited opportunities to use new physical and motor abilities; lack of affection, attention, and guidance; harsh, punishing discipline; unstable or insecure relationships with parents or other attachment persons; excessive teasing; and too few opportunities to play with other children. All these experiences interfere with healthy development of self-awareness, self-concept, and self-esteem.

> *Adults communicate unconditional acceptance when they honor children's feelings and perspectives, and support their competence and worth, while placing limits on inappropriate behaviors.*

Gender Identity and Gender Role Development

Four- and five-year-olds continue to learn gender role behaviors by noticing which of their masculine or feminine behaviors are encouraged and rewarded and which are punished. Children also learn gender-role expectations through classmates, playmates, mass media, children's literature, and classroom environments. Kohlberg (1966) suggests three development stages for establishing gender roles:

1. *Gender identity:* when children can identify themselves as boys or girls. This usually happens by age three.
2. *Gender stability:* when children realize that boys grow up to be men and girls grow up to be women. Gender stability usually occurs around age four.
3. *Gender constancy:* when children realize that changes in hairstyle or clothing do not change a person's gender. Gender constancy emerges between ages five and seven.

Before children achieve gender stability, their pretend play is not gender specific; for example, boys can be mothers, and girls can be fathers. Such behavior is normal and simply allows children to confirm their own gender identity and gender roles.

Four- and five-year-olds continue to have a lot of curiosity about their bodies and about the differences between girls and boys and between adults and children. They want to know where babies come from and why girls and boys have different bodies.

The developmental goal for parents, child care professionals, and other caregivers during this time is to help children develop healthy attitudes about their bodies and the concept of personal privacy. Caregivers need to give children accurate names for anatomy, information they can understand, and simple but *accurate* answers to questions. Adults should respond to each situation in a respectful and matter-of-fact way. This is not a time to punish or warn children; reprimands in such situations may convey an inaccurate message about human sexuality. At the same time, because curiosity is typical at this age, it is important for caregivers to help children understand the appropriate time and place for conversations about sexual topics. Child care professionals need to set clear limits regarding appropriate language, sexual play, nudity, touching, and being touched by others—and then monitor those limits consistently.

It is not uncommon for children who have been sexually abused to act out in provocative ways. They may use explicit language, be more intrusive with playmates, fondle them, or attempt oral contact or penetration. However, even these extreme behaviors can represent mere curiosity. Still, if you suspect sexual abuse, you must act to protect the child from further abuse. It is the law in all states that suspected child abuse *must* be reported to appropriate local and state officials. Child care settings and schools have policies and procedures for reporting child abuse.

> *The developmental goal for parents, child care professionals, and other caregivers during this time is to help children develop healthy attitudes about their bodies and the concept of personal privacy.*

Awareness of Diversity and Individual Differences

As children become aware of differing physical characteristics, gender, and abilities, they may behave toward one another in a variety of ways, including expressions of curiosity, friendship, hostility, or nervousness. They may touch each other's hair, compare skin colors, or ask questions. Children's perceptions of others are based on their limited experiences with people—doctors, dentists, babysitters, teachers, neighbors, playmates, and media personalities. As a result, they tend to believe that what is true of these people, according to their own experiences, is true of everyone.

Children can learn negative stereotypes from listening to their parents or other adults. They form ideas about people from portrayals in books, on television, in advertising, and so on. Children exposed to television news will note the color of the people being arrested in handcuffs and the color of the police officers. All these images, distorted or not, affect their perceptions of people and their place in the world. In other words, from birth onward, children grow up in a culture that molds their concepts and attitudes about race, cultural identity, moral values, and expectations.

Early child care, preschool, and kindergarten experiences can either support or contradict children's perceptions of race—both their own race and that of others. Early childhood programs can increase a child's growing sense of membership in a particular cultural or racial group and can encourage interest in, and respect for, other groups by doing the following:

- supporting the development of self-concept and cultural identity
- helping children develop the social skills of perspective-taking, communicating, cooperating, and solving conflicts
- expanding children's awareness of different lifestyles, languages, points of view, and ways of doing things through activities that introduce children to other cultures (Ramsey 1998)

Curricula that are *culturally responsive* recognize the racial and cultural mix in a given class or group of children, and provide experiences and information that respect diverse beliefs and value systems, traditions, family practices, and cultural histories.

Friendship and Play

Play is an important way for children to make new friends and develop social knowledge and skills. At this age, children are becoming more skilled at both *associative* and *cooperative play*, and they aren't as happy playing by themselves anymore.

In associative play, children share and talk about materials and activities, but each player explores and uses the materials in an individual way. Associative play may involve following another child around, imitating or getting ideas from other children's play, or talking with another child or children. However, each child's own ideas about how to play are still more important than other children's ideas. They want the activity to be done "their" way.

Cooperative play, on the other hand, is a sign of children's growing ability to recognize the ideas of others and to bring those ideas into their play. They plan and organize their play ideas together. Who gets to play and who doesn't is decided by certain members of the group. Cooperative play involves a higher level of social-interaction skill, including problem solving, accepting leader and follower roles, trying to understand play-mates' ideas and requests, being willing to change, and sharing creativity and responsibilities.

In Miriam Cohen's (1967) sensitive children's book *Will I Have a Friend?* Jim asks his father while en route to his first day at preschool, "Will I have a friend?" His father answers, "I think you will." This question is quite typical for children entering preschool or a new playgroup. It is also a sign of a very important part of psychosocial development: beginning and keeping friendships.

Relating effectively with others is an important part of being a social person. Becoming socially competent with peers involves developing certain skills: initiating interactions, keeping relationships, and solving conflicts (Asher, Renshaw, and Hymel 1982).

Some children are simply better at meeting other children. They're good at suggesting group activities or starting conversations. They seem to know how to wait for the right opportunity to join in, and they are also less noticeable and create fewer disruptions as they join children who are already playing. Other children may be more uncertain about how to meet new children, and may have trouble joining playgroups.

Friendships among four- and five-year-olds differ from toddlers'. Toddlers' friendships tend to be temporary: today's best friend may not be a friend at all tomorrow. For four- and five-year-olds, friendships last longer. During play, however, conflict may arise over the use of a toy or how some activity should proceed, and a friendship may be quickly ended—only to start up again a bit later.

In general, friendships at this age depend on being physically near one another, and sharing activities and toys. In young children, bargaining for friendships ("I'll be your friend if you let me hold your doll") and threatening ("If you don't give me one of those trucks, I won't ever, ever be your friend!") are common. Once friendships start, they are always in danger of ending over some disagreement. Children this age simply don't have the social behavior skills, the language ability, or the social knowledge they need to keep friendships going.

In order to develop strong social skills, young children need many opportunities to interact in different situations. Such opportunities include being in other people's homes, in preschool settings, in neighborhood playgroups, in family gatherings, and so on. While parents and teachers provide important guidance for children's developing social skills, children also benefit cognitively and socially from opportunities to interact with other children with little adult interaction. Especially in child care and classroom situations, staff should organize activities and materials that promote both cognitive growth and social skills.

Self-Control and Compliance

Studies of child-rearing practices have given child development researchers much insight into the kind of adult–child interactions that will most likely result in self-control, cooperation, and obedience in children. When infants and toddlers have developed a warm, mutually affectionate relationship with their caregivers, and when those caregivers are affectionate and are responsive, and use positive methods of guidance and control, children are more likely to obey requests.

On the other hand, children whose parents use arbitrary commands, physical control, or forceful actions are less likely to cooperate with other adults, regardless of how gentle or friendly those adults are. Caregivers and early childhood teachers may find it difficult to build a spirit of cooperation and compliance within the group.

Guidance techniques fall into three types: *Inductive discipline* gives children reasons for classroom rules that include logical limits for behavior and reasonable and logical consequences for disobedience. *Power-assertive discipline* uses force in the form of unreasonable and illogical threats (such as time away from the group or withdrawal of love), the removal of toys and privileges, mocking comments, or physical force or punishment. *Permissive discipline* tends to ignore inappropriate behaviors and generally fails to teach appropriate ones.

SUPPORTING SELF-CONTROL AND COMPLIANCE IN FOUR- AND FIVE-YEAR-OLDS

1. Provide an environment in which children's new ideas and motivation can grow and flourish. Such an environment includes these guidelines:
   a. enough space for the use of toys, equipment, and creative materials
   b. developmentally appropriate play items and activities that promote success and build self-confidence and self-esteem
   c. low, open shelves for storing personal work and play materials
   d. engaging, interesting, and challenging play items that encourage decision making, sharing, and cooperating
   e. safe furniture, play items, and surroundings
2. Provide a place where it's physically and psychologically safe for children to explore, experiment, and ask questions.

3. Provide opportunities to interact with other children that allow them to:
   a. share and problem-solve with other children their age
   b. create "plays" with other children that imitate the life they see around them
4. Establish a regular daily schedule. This helps children develop a sense of time that allows them to get ready for and participate in the day's activities. Such a schedule would have these qualities:
   a. meets children's physiological needs for food, water, rest, and exercise
   b. changes activities and expectations to fit children's short but growing attention spans
   c. provides advance notice of a need to change from one event to another
   d. allows time for children to finish the tasks or projects they're working on
   e. avoids long waiting times
5. Involve children in the setting of rules, limits, and standards for behavior. Here are some examples:
   a. set simple rules that are few in number, truly necessary, and focused on the most crucial behaviors. The three Ds of discipline are a good place to start (see the next point).
   b. set rules that help children recognize things that are *dangerous*, *destructive*, and/or *disturbing* or hurtful to others. Rules should always be stated in a positive way, telling children *what* to do rather than *what not* to do.
   c. explain the reasons behind the rules and encourage children to discuss logical consequences and the need for returning favors and help.
   d. assign age-appropriate chores and responsibilities, with adult assistance if needed. Chores can include returning personal items to assigned places, tidying the room or toy shelves, watering nontoxic houseplants, or caring for a pet.

Authoritative versus Authoritarian Approaches to Discipline

It's important to understand the differences between various approaches to discipline.

Authoritative guidance gives children reasonable and logical limits in a respectful, instructive, consistent, and predictable manner. Research shows that children of authoritative parents are more self-reliant, friendlier, have more self-control, and are more cooperative. Their children also tend to be more curious and optimistic and better able to handle stress than other children. Authoritative guidance is associated with advanced moral development. More recent studies found that these children had fewer risk-related behaviors during adolescence and were less likely to experiment with or abuse drugs.

Authoritarian discipline, on the other hand, is power-assertive and controlling. Obedience is expected, usually without explanation. Authoritarian adults may use coercive, punishing, forceful, and/or other negative techniques to maintain rules or limits. Studies show that children who experience authoritarian guidance are moodier, unhappy, and easily annoyed. They are more likely to show passive aggression or hostility, are less friendly, and are more vulnerable to stress.

Where *permissive discipline* is used, guidelines, limits, and instruction are mostly missing. Studies show that children who experience little or no guidance are the least self-controlled and self-reliant. They are more impulsive, aggressive, and rebellious. They are lower achievers compared to children who experience more positive and instructive forms of guidance.

Guidance techniques have both short-term and long-term goals and consequences. Meeting short-term goals may require quick thinking and action by adults to protect children and others. Short-term "fixes" (for example, taking away the toy truck to stop the possession argument; using a time-out chair for a child who used inappropriate words; separating chatty friends; providing candy for putting toys where they belong) seldom give children the thinking or the social tools they need to learn to control their behavior. Caregivers need to talk with children about prevention, about making amends for harm they've caused, and about limits and why they exist. Taking time to help children learn these lessons will benefit them enormously.

Guidance Goals for Young Children

Short-Term Goals

1. Protect children from endangering themselves or others, which includes limiting risky behaviors, preventing or calming anger, and preventing and resolving conflicts.

2. Reduce behaviors that are disruptive or disturbing to others, which includes respecting the privacy of others, respecting the personal space of others (including the visual and auditory space), and preventing the destruction of property (belonging to the child or to others).

Long-Term Goals

1. Establish positive self-concepts and self-confidence.
2. Develop self-direction and self-regulation.
3. Develop prosocial perspectives and behaviors, which includes strengthening problem-solving skills, learning to take another's point of view, and increasing one's capacity for empathy and altruism.
4. Develop character and morality.
5. Gain autonomy in choices and decision making.

Social and Moral Competence

Jeremy brings to kindergarten a large watercolor painting set that his parents bought him yesterday. He proudly shows it to some of his classmates. Many of them ask to play with him and if he'd share the water paints. Since the water paints are still new to him, Jeremy says, "No, not now! No one can use my paint set." He then goes off to a table to work alone with his paints. One or two classmates follow him to the table and continue to ask to work with him. Finally, Jeremy agrees. "Okay, Madeline, you can paint with me, but Joey, you can't paint with us. Maybe tomorrow I will let you paint."

Toys from the play center regularly seem to find their way into the bathroom and stay there until the teacher goes to get them. Besides getting dirty, the toys are "lost" for others who want to play with them. Angela's teacher organizes a class meeting to discuss the situation. After explaining her concerns, she asks the class to help her find a solution to this problem.

Thomas says that whoever is doing that should "get a spanking." Geraldo says that if the toys are really lost or too dirty to play with, his daddy will buy new toys. Katie suggests that if they get dirty, her mommy can wash them. Rashid begs the teacher to throw the toys away "because they might be really, really, really dirty!"

The teacher tries to bring the children back to the main problem: responsibility for the care of classroom materials. "You have made some interesting suggestions and have been very thoughtful; we all appreciate that. However, I am still wondering if there is something we can do right here in our classroom and not involve people who are not here with us every day."

Carson suggests, "We could wash our own toys in the sand and water table."

Then Angela, after careful thinking and listening, suggests, "We can put a sign on the toilet door that says 'No toys allowed' to remind everybody not to take toys in there." Her classmates agree and talk about who will make the sign.

The teacher thanks Angela and asks, "Is there anything else we can do?" Angela, with no more ideas left, says, "Well! They will just have to remember not to do that."

Both of these vignettes illustrate different levels of social competence. Jeremy is self-confident and curious with his new set of paints. He's aware of others' desires to paint with him, but he's still learning to share. Angela, on the other hand, shows strong cooperative and problem-solving skills. She's confident in her ability to share solutions and she shows a beginning awareness of morally responsible behavior.

WHAT IS SOCIAL COMPETENCE?

Social competence is the growing awareness of others and choosing whether or not to interact with other people. It includes the ability to initiate interactions, to carry on conversations, and to continue relationships. How children feel about their interactions affects how much they will seek them out.

The culture in which children grow up teaches them values, beliefs, customs, and social skills that have been passed along from one generation to the next. Parents are generally the main people responsible for socializing young children, along with siblings and other family members, family friends, and neighbors. Young children are also socialized by experiences in child care and preschool settings, faith-based affiliations, and other groups. They develop social concepts and behaviors by watching and interacting with people and by watching television and interacting with other media. Social development, self-regard, awareness of diversity, and ideas about gender, self-control, and moral development all affect children's growing ability to make and keep friendships and to have positive interactions with others.

Social competence includes the following:

• the ability to regulate emotions

- having enough social knowledge and understanding to form friendships
- the ability to recognize and respond appropriately to social cues in others and to use language to interact effectively
- having certain social skills, such as understanding ways to meet new people, giving positive attention to others, being able to have conversations with others, and taking turns
- having qualities that are needed for effective social relationships, such as cooperativeness, responsibility, and empathy (Katz and McClellan 1997)

In chapter 6, you'll learn the factors that affect psychosocial development, including interactions within and outside the family and the role played by individual temperament and personality.

References

Asher, S. R., P. D. Renshaw, and S. Hymel. 1982. Peer relations and the development of social skills. In *The young child: Reviews of research*, vol. 3, ed. S. G. Moore and C. R. Cooper, 137–158. Washington, D.C.: National Association for the Education of Young Children.

Cohen, Miriam. 1967. *Will I have a friend?* New York: Macmillan.

Katz, L. G., and D. E. McClellan. 1997. *Fostering children's social competence: The teacher's role*. Washington, D.C.: National Association for the Education of Young Children.

Kohlberg, L. 1966. A cognitive-developmental analysis of children's sex-role concepts and attitudes. In *The development of sex differences*, ed. E. E. Maccoby, 82–173. Stanford, Calif.: Stanford University Press.

Ramsey, P. G. 1998. *Teaching and learning in a diverse world: Multicultural education for young children*. 2nd ed. New York: Teachers College Press.

6 Factors Influencing Psychosocial Development

Factors that affect psychosocial development include:

- a child's unique personality and temperament
- the extent of support given to help develop a sense of initiative
- the extent of support given to address special and developmental needs
- the types of interactions a child has with family members and others
- the way the child has been cared for and taught by caregivers
- a child's relationships with siblings and friends
- television and exposure to other media

Individual Temperament and Personality

From birth, infants have personalities. As a child ages, she develops a unique way of feeling, thinking, and interacting with others. *Temperament* is the term generally used to describe these unique qualities. Researchers Stella Chess and Alexander Thomas (1987, 1996) have identified three main types of temperament:

1. *The easy temperament*. These children are usually easygoing, even tempered, accepting of change, playful, open, and adaptable. Their eating and sleeping schedules are quite regular,

they are easily comforted when upset, and they generally are in a good mood.

2. *The difficult temperament.* These children are slow to develop regular eating and sleeping routines, are more irritable, get less pleasure from playtime activities, have difficulty adjusting to changes in routines, and tend to cry louder and longer than more easily soothed children.

3. *The slow-to-warm-up temperament.* These children show only mild positive or negative reactions; they don't like new situations and new people; they are moody and slow to adapt. The slow-to-warm-up child may resist close interactions such as cuddling.

Although temperament may be genetically determined, it clearly affects and is affected by the environment.

As with other types of growth and development, a child's temperament also affects his psychosocial development. New studies of the relationship between the personalities of children and their caregivers expand on this idea. Child development experts now think that parents and children alike have behaviors that bring out expected responses in each other, for example, the rebellious child and the overly rigid parent.

In addition to temperament, other personal characteristics affect the kinds of responses children get from others. Physical appearance, ideas about attractiveness, health, vitality, cleanliness, and grooming can all affect a child's self-concept and can produce behaviors that are either positive and prosocial or negative and difficult.

Supporting Initiative

Caregivers can encourage children to develop initiative by giving them opportunities to explore and to try new and challenging activities. Four- and five-year-olds would benefit a lot from the resultant cooperative activities and the projects that make them think in new ways.

Materials that children can use to build, color, and paint, for example, as well as space and props for imaginative play, help them develop a sense of initiative by letting them express their ideas. Age-appropriate toys, learning materials, and opportunities for social interaction can teach children to trust their ideas and take initiative. Adults can support this growth by talking with them about what they're doing, answering their *how* and *why* questions, allowing them to make choices, helping them to think about what they make, and anticipating ways in which children can share or take full responsibility for an activity or event.

As children succeed with a project or task, they better understand how they can participate in and contribute to an activity or event. Figuring out particular interests and skills will help you select the types of activities and interactions that will work best for each child.

Supporting Special Needs

Many types of disabling conditions affect young children, with varying degrees of severity. The special needs of children generally fall into three categories:

1. Developmental delays: children who demonstrate delays in one or more of the following developmental domains:
   a. *physical/motor:* growth rates that are quite different from the norm for the child's age; differences in large- or small-motor control or in speaking ability
   b. *self-help skills:* difficulties in dressing, feeding, or using a toilet without assistance
   c. *social-emotional behaviors:* attachment problems, difficulty controlling emotions, and problems with social interactions
   d. *communication:* limited use of language to communicate and the inability to understand or respond to communications with others
   e. *cognitive development:* limited curiosity and interest in learning, lack of focus, difficulty learning, or unusual play behaviors or play themes
2. Atypical development: children whose patterns of development are different from those of their peers, including the following:
   a. *sensorimotor differences:* poor muscle tone, abnormal reflex activity, and sensory impairments
   b. *unusual social-emotional patterns:* unusual attachment behaviors, unusual social responses and expressions of emotions, or self-injurious behaviors
   c. *atypical cognitive and language development:* the inability to focus and pay attention, learning and memory difficulties, difficulties associated with the learning, and difficulties processing information
3. Medically diagnosed conditions: children with various possible diagnoses, including aphasia (profound lack of language), cerebral palsy, congenital muscular dystrophy, Down

syndrome, drug withdrawal syndrome, failure to thrive, fetal alcohol syndrome, seizure disorders, and spinal cord injury

Children with special needs are at greater risk of having socialization problems, such as shyness, withdrawal, and lack of skill starting friendships and activities. In fact, for children with learning disabilities, it's *common* to have problems socializing. Developing self-concept, self-esteem and prosocial behavior and making friends can be particularly difficult. For hearing-impaired children, making friends is particularly difficult because other kids and adults think they're unfriendly.

> *Children with special needs can benefit from a teacher or other adult who helps them learn the social behaviors they need to interact successfully with others.*

Special-needs children may also have difficulty with gaining perspective. This can prevent them from recognizing and thinking about others' feelings and viewpoints. Consider children who can't see well and feel rejected. The real problem is in their lack of facial or other nonverbal cues that indicate friendliness (such as smiling) and thus encourage other kids to talk or play with them.

Children with special needs will benefit from a teacher or other adult who helps them learn the social behaviors they need to interact successfully with others. On the other end, helping children *without* special needs accept and interact with children *with* special needs is essential. Because young children are curious and often quite frank, teachers should simply give accurate but reassuring information about children and their disabilities. Teachers should provide opportunities for all children to interact together and should monitor play and work behaviors for opportunities to promote prosocial interactions.

Meeting the Needs of Children with Disabilities

Today, federal laws order early screening and identification of children with disabilities. As a child care professional, you play a vital role in this process. You may, in fact, be the first to notice a developmental problem in a child in your care. Early diagnosis can help families begin getting children the extra help they need as soon as possible. Intervention services for young children with special needs include access to some or all of the following:

- Early identification
- Screening and assessment

- assistive technology
- vision and hearing evaluation and follow-up services
- family counseling
- medical and health care services
- home visits
- nutrition supervision
- physical therapy
- psychological services
- speech and language therapy
- transportation

Since screening for at-risk children has become more common, the potential for its abuse has become a concern. Child care workers stress the importance of using accurate screening methods and of using qualified professionals to screen and diagnose young children. It is important that programs to which children are assigned meet professional standards of quality and developmental appropriateness. They must also serve the best long-term interest of the child. When the decision is made to place a child with special needs in an inclusive classroom, her family, teachers, and other resource staff must work together to prepare the classroom and curricula to help the child feel included and accepted.

INCLUSIVE PRACTICES

Including children with disabilities is both an opportunity and a challenge for early childhood programs and professionals. First, planning for the safety of all children and preparing to meet the requirements of children with special needs are essential to successful inclusion practices. Second, as an early childhood professional, it's important that you establish effective and ongoing communication with parents and other professionals who are involved in the care and education of children with special needs.

You may need to change the classroom layout or make other arrangements to make it easier for children with special needs to use and enjoy materials and activities. Children with visual or hearing difficulties will likely need adjustments in seating and in the design and placement of classroom visual materials (bulletin boards, charts, art displays, and so on). Toilet areas, shelving, and storage space for personal things should be reexamined. Furniture arrangements and pathways need to be organized for the use of crutches, walkers, wheelchairs, or other assistive equipment.

Special dietary requirements should be considered in classroom food and nutrition lessons, snacks, parties, and other food-related events.

It's also important to pay close attention to daily health routines—medications, meals and snacks, access to drinking water, toileting, rest and exercise, personal hygiene, and classroom cleanliness and order. The social and intellectual climate of the classroom should be accepting, comfortable, and psychologically safe. Each adult plays an important role in modeling and teaching good health habits, as well as acceptance and respect for all individuals.

Familial and Extrafamilial Interactions

Although four- and five-year-olds are becoming more independent, self-sufficient, and eager to interact and play with their peers, they still depend on adults for support and guidance as they explore an ever-widening social world. Four- and five-year-olds continue to need and want intimacy and affection, communication and companionship, encouragement and assistance, and assurances and affirmation from those who care for them. Children also want and expect adults to protect them from harm, provide positive guidance and leadership, and teach or help them discover acceptable and effective social behaviors and ways to express their emotions. As children try to understand their feelings and desires and try to control their behaviors and interactions, they watch how the adults in their lives behave—and then imitate what they see.

> *Angela is setting the table in the home-living center at kindergarten. Her friend, Jason, joins her and proceeds to pour water in the cups for "hot chocolate." The two then sit down and begin to drink. Suddenly, Angela stops and tells Jason, "You have to put your napkin in your lap first." A bit confused, Jason asks, "Why?" "Because that's the way my mama does it," says Angela.*

As illustrated by Angela's behavior, young children *carefully* watch the interactions and responses, both verbal and nonverbal, of adults who care for them. They are often even more aware of the words and actions of those with whom they have close and warm relationships, such as parents and child care providers. Children will imitate these behaviors and eventually such behaviors become part of a child's natural responses.

Peer Relationships

Obviously, young children enjoy the company of their friends. As with adults, four- and five-year-olds learn behaviors—both good and bad—from their friends. Peer groups are a kind of testing ground for children to try out different behaviors and interactions. Adults, however, still have the most influence on them.

Television and Technology

Children today enjoy the products of an ever-changing and expanding electronics industry. Television remains the most used electronic tool; it has been a topic of concern and research for decades. In addition, computers, video equipment, and electronic toys and devices are finding their way into more and more U.S. homes and, like television, are being closely examined by child development and early education researchers.

Much research on the negative effects of television on children's behavior has examined violence and aggression, inadequate and inappropriate gender and cultural role models, and the effects of advertising directed at young children. Other studies have tried to identify the positive influences of television: for example, how it affects language development, literacy, general knowledge, and behavior.

The effects of television, video games, assorted electronic toys, and other devices on psychosocial development depend on a number of factors, including the amount of time spent using them, the amount of time spent engaged in other healthy and productive activities, the content and quality of the programs and games, and the attitudes and values of those using these technologies. Time spent watching television, of course, takes time away from physical activities that are so important for children's motor development and physical fitness. Fewer opportunities to interact with friends, parents, and others clearly interfere with healthy psychosocial development.

Because children learn best through interacting with other humans, too much time alone in front of television or computer screens can diminish cognitive and social development. Children want and need real responses from other human beings to help them make sense of their experiences, and the overuse of electronic media can interfere with these human connections. In addition, children's limited abilities to understand the difference between fantasy and reality often make the content of television, video games, and other electronic media confusing and misleading.

Worries about prejudice, violence, aggression, crudeness, and explicit sex in media programs and video games have prompted many studies of the long-term effects of using these technologies. Many groups concerned with children's care and well-being have tried to limit programming that we know encourages children to imitate antisocial behavior. The American Psychological Association estimates that by the time children finish elementary school, they will have seen about 8,000 televised murders and 100,000 other acts of violence. Responding to increasing concern about violence in the media, the governing board of the National Association for the Education of Young Children (NAEYC) has published a position statement and a teachers' guide condemning violent television programming, movies, videotapes, computer games, and other forms of media to which young children are exposed (NAEYC 1995).

> *By the time children finish elementary school, they will have seen about 8,000 televised murders and 100,000 other acts of violence.*

Child development researchers are also concerned about behaviors that television and other electronic media discourage. Time spent in front of screens is time *not* spent interacting with family members—talking, arguing, playing games, and taking part in family festivities—activities researchers know are essential for learning and building character.

Some programs, however, *do* promote positive social behaviors and understanding, and children and families can be guided toward such programs. Regular exposure to such programming has been shown to positively influence children's behavior. However, viewing alone does not guarantee positive behaviors. Children need adults to help them talk about what they've seen, to understand a program's topics and role models, and to encourage them to use in their daily lives the positive behaviors of the characters they like.

References

Chess, S., and A. Thomas. 1987. *Origins and evolution of behavior disorders from infancy to early adult life.* Cambridge, Mass.: Harvard University Press.

————. 1996. *Temperament: Theory and practice.* New York: Brunner/Mazel.

National Association for the Education of Young Children. 1995. Media violence and children: A guide for parents. Washington, D.C.: NAEYC.

The Role of the Early Childhood Professional

1. Support children's continuing need to be lovingly cared for and secure.
2. Support children's emerging sense of self and provide experiences and interactions that support self-esteem.
3. Model and teach positive social behaviors.
4. Encourage children to try new activities and behaviors while still providing safe, reasonable limits.
5. Help children understand and cope with fear, anger, and other emotions.
6. Through discussion and role playing, facilitate the development of perspective.
7. Provide authoritative and instructive discipline.
8. Encourage interesting productive play and interactions with other children.
9. Support positive relationships with other children by minimizing comparisons and competition and by encouraging individuality.
10. Respond respectfully and with interest to children's questions about gender, race, and diversity, and provide unbiased and informative answers.

Discussion Questions

1. Do you give the preschoolers in your program daily responsibilities? What tasks might they participate in or accomplish on their own to help them feel more independent and boost their confidence level? Develop a preschooler "task list" that changes from week to week, allowing preschoolers to experience a variety of responsibilities. Teach them to make a check mark next to their name on the task list once they've completed their task for the day.

2. As noted in chapter 4, preschoolers learn a lot by watching the adults in their life and by role playing. Observe how the children in your program interact while role playing and make a mental note of issues to talk about during circle time or story time. For example, if the children are behaving inappropriately during a birthday-party role play, read a book about attending a birthday party during story time, and then talk with the children as a group about appropriate party behavior.

3. Chapters 5 and 6 discuss how adults can help preschoolers develop perspective-taking abilities and learn to label emotions. In what ways do you introduce the concepts of emotions and empathy to preschoolers in your program? In what ways do you help them learn to manage emotions?

4. Chapter 6 lists different types of disciplinary and guidance techniques. What sorts of techniques have you found to be most effective with the children in your care? Do you modify the technique depending on the personality traits of the child being disciplined or do you use the same technique with every child?

Further Reading

American Academy of Pediatrics. Some things you should know about media violence and media literacy. http://www.aap.org/advocacy/child-healthmonth/media.htm.

Bell, S. H., V. W. Carr, D. Denno, L. J. Johnson, and L. R. Phillips. 2004. *Challenging behaviors in early childhood settings: Creating a place for all children*. Baltimore: Brookes Publishing Co.

DeVries, R., and B. Zan. 1994. *Moral classrooms, moral children: Creating a constructivist atmosphere in early education*. New York: Teachers College Press.

Elkind, D. 2001. *The hurried child: Growing up too fast too soon*. New York: Perseus Books Publishing Co.

Hopkins, S. 1999. *Hearing everyone's voice: Educating young children for peace and democratic community*. Redmond, Wash.: Child Care Information Exchange.

Kaiser, B., and J. S. Rasminsky. 1999. *Meeting the challenge: Effective strategies for challenging behaviours in early childhood environments*. Ottawa: Canadian Child Care Federation.

Katz, L. G., and D. E. McClellan. 1997. *Fostering children's social competence: The teacher's role*. Washington, D.C.: National Association for the Education of Young Children.

Kemple, K. M. 2004. *Let's be friends: Peer competence and social inclusion in early childhood programs*. New York: Teachers College Press.

Levin, D. E. 2003. *Teaching young children in violent times*. 2nd ed. Washington, D.C.: National Association for the Education of Young Children.

Lowenthal, B. 2001. *Abuse and neglect: The educator's guide to the identification and prevention of child maltreatment*. Baltimore: Brookes Publishing Co.

Rideout, V. I., E. A. Vanderwater, and E. A. Wartella. 2003. *Zero to six: Electronic media in the lives of infants, toddlers and preschoolers*. Menlo Park, CA: Henry J. Kaiser Family Foundation.

Other Resources

- American Academy of Child and Adolescent Psychiatry Facts for Families. http://www.aacap.org/

- ERIC: Clearinghouse on Elementary and Early Childhood Education University of Illinois
51 Gerty Drive
Champaign, IL 61820-7469
217-333-1386
ERIC digests (concise one-page articles and reports on timely issues) include the following:
Marion, M. 1997. *Helping young children deal with anger.* EDO-PS-97-24.
McClellan, D. E., and L. G. Katz. 1993. *Young children's social development: A checklist.* EDO-PS-93-6.

Part Three

Cognitive, Language, and Literacy Development

Was it not then that I acquired all that now sustains me? And I gained so much and so quickly that during the rest of my life I did not acquire a hundredth part of it. From myself as a five-year-old to myself as I now am there is only one step. The distance between myself as an infant and myself at five years is tremendous.

—LEO TOLSTOY

Cognitive development is quite rapid in the first eight years of life. In the first two books in this series, we looked at how both biology and environment affect cognitive development. At first, cognitive development is dominated by children's sensory and motor abilities, but it also affects and is affected by growth and development in other areas—physical, emotional, social, language, and literacy.

Part 3 of *Understanding Preschooler Development* examines the cognitive development of four- and five-year-olds. It begins with a look at theories of cognitive, language, and literacy development, including a review of Howard Gardner's theory of multiple intelligences. You'll learn how language development and communication affect every part of children's development—social interactions, cognitive development, emotional intelligence, and cultural competence. You'll also learn how children become aware of print and learn to write, and how you can recognize early reading behavior and support literacy development. Finally, you'll explore the major factors that influence cognitive, language, and literacy development, including nutrition, health, and enrollment in preschool programs.

7 Theories of Cognitive Development

Among the different theories of cognitive development in young children, three have risen to prominence: constructivism (Jean Piaget), multiple intelligences (Howard Gardner), and the social interactionist perspective.

Constructivism

According to the constructivist theory of Swiss child development psychologist Jean Piaget, children under age six or seven are in the preoperational stage of development. This means that they are not fully capable of complicated thinking or logical reasoning. Piaget came to his conclusions about this stage in children's thinking after doing a number of experiments. In one experiment, a liquid is poured from a tall, slender container into a short, wide one; in another experiment, a ball of clay is rolled into a long, thin rope. Preoperational thinkers judge the amount of the liquid and the clay by its appearance (tall is more; long is more). In fact, they do this even when they have seen the liquid poured from one container into the other and back, or when the clay is rolled from a ball into a rope and then back to its original shape. The process of transformation is complex for children at this age. They generally do not apply the concept of *conservation*—understanding that the physical features of an object or substance remain the same even if its shape changes—until they are at least seven years old.

Piaget explained this inability to understand the process of conservation by looking at young children's behaviors in a number of experiments. He found that preoperational children tended to focus on specific events rather than on the process of change. They neither have the ability to reason inductively (to shift their thinking from the specific to the general), nor the ability to move from the general to the specific. In addition, preoperational thinking is controlled by perceptions, that is, preoperational ideas are based on how things are sensed—how they appear, sound, and feel. If the amount of water *looks* taller, then the preoperational child will decide there is more of it.

As children move through the preoperational stage, they gradually begin to solve conservation problems by playing and experimenting with actual objects and then by counting, measuring, and using basic logic. As they get older, they won't have to rely as often on actual experiences to solve conservation problems. However, they may continue to do so throughout the schooling years as a way to help them understand problems.

In addition to using perception-bound thinking, preoperational children are not able to "reverse" their thinking and return to the start of a thought. This irreversibility is the key difference between the thinking of preoperational children and the thinking of older children and adults. For example: The same number of objects is placed in two parallel rows of the same length. Then, as children watch, the objects in one row are spread out so that this row appears longer than the other row. If you ask preoperational children which row has more objects, they will point to the longer row. They aren't able to think back to the beginning of the experiment—when there were two rows of the same length with the same number of objects—so they don't understand that both rows have the same number of objects, even though they watched a short row change.

If children ages two to three are asked to group objects that belong together (blocks, for example), they are generally unable to do so. Not until sometime between ages four and six do children begin to group and classify objects on the basis of their qualities, such as color, shape, size, and function. However, they still may forget the quality they were using to classify the objects. Late in the preoperational period, children *can* classify objects based on their qualities.

Another interesting difference between the thinking of early and later preoperational children is *transivity*, that is, the ability to put objects in order according to their size, height, color, or some other quality. Children ages two to three generally cannot arrange a series of objects from shortest to longest. Older preoperational children can do this, but they cannot arrange objects *representationally*, that is, they can't do this activity "in their head." Instead, they must use actual objects.

Still another thought process that develops during the preoperational stage is *identity constancy*. This is the understanding that the identity and characteristics of a person or species remain the same even though its appearance can be changed with masks or costumes.

> *Angela, at age four, visits a toy store with her grandmother. There they encounter a friend and neighbor who is a salesperson at the store; she is dressed as a storybook character. Angela hides behind her grandmother and peeks out in fear of the costumed person. Even though the voice behind the mask is familiar, Angela doesn't relax until she and her grandmother have left the store to return home.*

In this vignette, Angela shows that she does not yet understand that a change in appearance does not fundamentally change a person's identity. She was unable to understand that the costumed salesperson was her neighbor. The following story about Jeremy shows that by the time children are five or six years old, they begin to understand that identity remains constant even though physical appearance is changed.

> *Shortly after Jeremy turns four, his grandmother comes to visit for several weeks. It is close to Halloween and Grandma wants to help make Jeremy's costume. Jeremy decides he wants to be a ghost. Ann finds an old white sheet and Grandma begins working on Jeremy's costume. At first, Jeremy seems quite excited about being a ghost for Halloween. However, as time goes on, he seems more and more unwilling to try on his costume.*
>
> *When Ann and Grandma pick up Jeremy at school on the day of the Halloween party, they ask Jeremy's teacher if he had worn his costume during the parade. Ms. Buckley says he had. Ann describes the change in Jeremy's behavior while the costume was being made. Jeremy's teacher then explains that, at this age, children have a difficult time understanding the difference between reality and fantasy. Jeremy was probably afraid he might actually become a ghost if he wore the costume.*
>
> *After Halloween, Ann puts the costume in a toy box, but Jeremy doesn't play with it.*
>
> *About a year later, Jeremy is taking all the toys out of his toy box*

when he finds the ghost costume. He puts it on and runs around the house shouting, "Boo!" From then on, Jeremy sometimes plays ghost. Ann thinks about what Ms. Buckley had said. She has noticed that when they are reading, Jeremy is beginning to talk about whether the story could "really happen."

These behaviors show that Jeremy is beginning to understand the idea of identity constancy and that he is better able to understand the difference between reality and fantasy.

While Piaget's theory has formed the foundation for thinking, research, and practice for more than fifty years, more recent research has identified weaknesses in the theory and has provided additional ways to view childhood thinking and learning. As with studies of children in general, this research process is a continuous one that promises to help us better understand human development.

Multiple Intelligences

Howard Gardner, in his multiple-intelligence theory, suggests that:

- There are many different kinds of minds.
- We learn, remember, understand, and perform in many different ways.
- We are capable of knowing things in different ways.

Gardner also proposes that humans have at least ten different intelligences:

1. *Intrapersonal intelligence:* the ability to detect and symbolize complex and very different sets of feelings
2. *Interpersonal intelligence:* the ability to recognize distinctions among other people's moods, temperaments, motivations, and intentions
3. *Spatial intelligence:* the ability to accurately see the world
4. *Bodily kinesthetic intelligence:* the ability to direct one's bodily motions and manipulate objects skillfully
5. *Musical intelligence:* exceptional awareness of pitch, rhythm, and timbre
6. *Linguistic intelligence:* sensitivity to meaning, order, sounds, rhythms, and inflections of words
7. *Logical-mathematical intelligence:* the ability to attend to patterns, categories, and relationships
8. *Naturalist intelligence:* the ability to recognize important differ-

ences in the natural world among plants and animals, natural phenomena, and changes over time

9. *Spiritual intelligence:* the ability to relate to the mysteries of life and death and to the "why" questions of human existence, the supernatural, and altered states of consciousness

10. *Existential intelligence:* a part of spiritual intelligence that includes the ability to locate oneself within the cosmos—the infinite—while dealing with such intellectual issues as the meaning of life and death, the ultimate fate of the physical and psychological worlds, or other mysterious or powerful life experiences

Rather than focus only on intellectual potential, Gardner believes that everyone has each of these intelligences in various combinations—and to greater or lesser amounts. Gardner's multiple-intelligence theory could have a major effect on anyone who works with children. He suggests that teachers and other caregivers should not ask "How smart are you?" but instead "In what ways are you smart?" This approach emphasizes individual strengths and uniquenesses. It also gives us a better idea of individual capabilities than traditional intelligence tests do.

> *Teachers and other caregivers should not ask "How smart are you?" but instead "In what ways are you smart?"*

Gardner gives child care professionals another way to look at cognitive, language, and literacy development. He shows how intelligence is closely connected to culture, needs, and experience (rather than gender, race, or socioeconomic background). For example, studies show that women in Western cultures do not perform as well on spatial tasks as men. However, in an environment where spatial orientation is important for survival (for example, among the Inuit, the indigenous people of the Arctic coasts, which are covered in snow and ice), women and men perform equally well on spatial tasks. Gardner also shows that experience, survival needs, and cultural expectations, including expectations about gender and race, *all* play roles in the types of intelligence that evolve within individual people and among and between culturally and geographically diverse groups of people. In the South Sea Islands, the Puluwat culture places a high value on spatial intelligence, which is necessary for navigating canoes to and from several hundred islands in the ocean. Children are taught from an early age to identify the constellations, the islands on the horizon, and the differences on the water surface.

Other cultures highly value musical intelligence. For example, children of the Anang tribe in Nigeria know hundreds of dances and songs by the time they're five years old. In the United States, schools place the heaviest emphasis on linguistic intelligence and logical-mathematical intelligence.

All cultures use combinations of intelligence. Too often, stereotypes about supposed racial or ethnic characteristics, such as athleticism, musical or rhythmic ability, or math and science skills, do not take this into account. In many school settings, making such assumptions has a negative effect on children who have strengths in other types of intelligence. It's important that teachers, parents, and child care professionals understand multiple-intelligence development and let children grow and develop in ways that support their strengths.

Social Interactionist Perspective

Another explanation of the differences in children's cognitive development looks at how children's experiences in their families, communities, and society affect the formation of roles. Young children often participate in routine events with adults over a period of time. Eventually children develop ideas about the roles people play in certain situations, about the objects or materials they use, and about the order of various events. For example, when playing Restaurant, children take time to decide on the roles: who will be the cook, the server, and the customer. Then children act out these various roles as they go to the restaurant, order, eat, pay for the food, and leave. Four- and five-year-olds often use appropriate props, such as real or pretend menus, ordering pads, pencils, dishes, pots and pans, tables, chairs, and cash registers. And as children mature, these plays imitate real life to a greater degree.

The idea of roles can also explain some of the differences in young children's abilities and behaviors. For example, children in some Asian cultures become very skilled at eating with chopsticks, doing origami (the art of paper folding), and other small-motor tasks because adults in the culture provide many opportunities for them to practice these skills. These skills may not be as important in other cultures. For that reason, children from other cultures may not have the opportunity to repeatedly practice the same small-motor tasks and so might not be as advanced in their small-motor development as children from some Asian cultures.

Even though none of these theories perfectly explains human cognitive development, we still can find in them some helpful ideas:

- Infants and children are neurologically wired to learn and are naturally motivated to do so.
- From infancy on, cognitive abilities change in number and

quality, in a somewhat predictable fashion, as brain growth and neurological development proceed.

- Cognitive development includes many mental processes, such as perception, attention, thinking, memory, problem solving, creativity, and communication.
- Cognition is affected by children's increasingly complex experiences and interactions with objects and events in the world around them.
- Language skills support children's thinking abilities.
- Developing the tools needed for learning—drawing, writing, spelling, reading, and basic math and science skills—helps advance cognition.
- Individuals have unique cognitive styles and intellectual abilities (that is, multiple intelligences at different strengths) that often can't be described or measured by traditional methods.
- Educational and academic successes can be traced back to the cognitive and social/emotional skills that preschoolers had when they began school, and to the kind of early childhood experiences that nourished these abilities.

The next chapter talks more about the amazing way that children develop language. You'll learn about indirect speech and when kids begin to understand it. You'll explore when and how children begin to understand riddles and look at children's word acquisition. Finally, you'll learn what steps you can take as a child care professional to support language development, and how to promote communicative competence.

8

Language Development

Language and communication affect every part of a child's development—social interactions, cognitive development, emotional intelligence, and cultural competence. The ability to use language well helps children communicate in relationships, makes learning easier, and aids in school success. If you have ever tried to learn another language or have visited a culture whose language you couldn't speak, you probably understand how difficult even the simplest tasks can be, such as shopping or asking for directions, without good language skills.

As children get older, their ability to remember more information supports their language development. As children experience more, they hear and learn vocabulary that fits different situations. This knowledge, together with a growing ability to put events in order, helps four- and five-year-olds develop more sophisticated and complex language skills. For example, they become much better at having longer conversations. You'll see examples of this new growth when you watch children's pretend play, in which they act out roles they've learned through new experiences, such as going to the doctor, eating out, or grocery shopping.

> *One evening, as Ann helps Jeremy out of the tub and dries his feet, she notices how much his feet are shaped like his father's. She says, "Jeremy, you sure have your daddy's feet." But Jeremy replies, "I do not have Daddy's feet. These are* my *feet!"*

Despite their growing competence, four- and five-year-olds still have a lot to learn about language and the exact meanings of words and phrases. In the above example, Jeremy simply didn't understand what we call *indirect speech*—speech that implies more than what the words actually say. What Ann meant, of course, was that Jeremy's feet were shaped like his father's feet, but Jeremy only understood the literal meaning of her statement.

Children begin to understand indirect speech around age four or five. At first, all young children take others' speech literally. However, as they move into the preschool years, they begin to experiment with humor and lying as forms of indirect speech. For example, children around age five begin to be interested in riddles and jokes. While young children's "jokes" often aren't funny to older children and adults, they usually elicit enthusiastic laughter from the joke teller. This is because preschoolers understand the *form* of jokes or riddles, and they know it's appropriate to laugh at a joke, but they don't understand that words can have more than one meaning. Preschoolers also gradually become aware of lying, but they're usually no better at lying than joke telling because they don't understand all the factors needed to create a believable lie.

Language and communication affect every part of a child's development—social interactions, cognitive development, emotional intelligence, and cultural competence.

Vocabulary Development

At twelve to eighteen months, children begin to acquire an amazing number of words. Some studies indicate that young children learn and remember an average of nine words a day from the time they begin speaking until age six. At that rate, by the time a child is six or seven, she will have acquired a vocabulary of approximately fourteen thousand words!

While many factors contribute to the learning and use of words, perhaps the most important have to do with the interactions children have with parents and caregivers. One ambitious and fascinating study of language development in young children showed that language development was overwhelmingly affected by the quantity and quality of the interactions between parents and children (Hart and Risley 1995). The researchers studied forty-two families with young children for two-and-a-half years, spending one hour per month with each family in the home, and recording and analyzing every word spoken between parents and children. The families were from three different socioeconomic groups: professional, working class, and welfare.

Hart and Risley found an astounding difference of almost three hundred words per hour between the professional and welfare parents. They then calculated that over a year's time: the children in the professional families heard approximately eleven million words per year, while the children in the working-class families heard six million and the children in the welfare families heard three million.

They also found that children's vocabulary growth was affected not only by the *number* of words children hear, but also by the vocabulary used,

> *By the time a child is six or seven, she will have acquired a vocabulary of approximately fourteen thousand words.*

the sentence structure used, the way parents responded to their children's speech, and the emotional quality of the interactions. Hart and Risley discovered that these indicators were associated not only with vocabulary development, but also with IQ scores (measured at age three). These factors were better predictors of differences among children than were race, gender, or birth order.

Hart and Risley made another critical finding, one that is important not only for language development, but also for psychosocial reasons: children in welfare families received more negative feedback in their language interactions with parents than children in the other two groups.

Other factors that affect vocabulary growth include the following:

- the number of times and ways that adults (parents, teachers, caregivers) define words and label objects, events, and feelings
- hearing the conversations of others
- watching or hearing spoken language in television, movies, videos, and other media
- listening to stories
- interacting with older siblings and playmates
- school instruction (although to a lesser extent than the other factors)

Syntax

As children enter their fourth year, conjunctions with *and* begin to appear in their speech (for example, "I want cookies *and* milk"). Later, conjunctions such as *because, so, if, or,* and *but* appear. The use of *when, then, before,* and *after* develops still later. During ages four and five, what are called embedded sentences, tag questions, indirect object–direct object constructions, and passive sentence forms also begin to appear. (See the numbered list on the next page.)

Definition: *Syntax*—the rules each language has about how to put words in sentence order and about the relationship between the words and other structural elements in phrases and sentences.

FORMS AND USAGE OF GRAMMAR FROM AGES FOUR THROUGH SIX

1. Conjunctions
   a. Using *and* to connect whole sentences:
      "My daddy picked me up at school *and* we went to the store."
      "We ate breakfast *and* we ate doughnuts, too!"
   b. Later, expressing relations between clauses using *because* and *if*:
      "I can't hold my cup *because* I'm too little."
      "I'll play with my new truck *if* my daddy brings it."
2. Embedded Sentences
   "I *want to hold it* myself!"
   "I *want to go to sleep* in my big-boy bed."
   "My mommy said *she could fix it*."
3. Tag Questions
   "I can do it myself, *can't I?*"
   "Caitlin is crying, *isn't she, Mommy?*"
   "Mommy, this shoe is too small, *isn't it, Daddy?*"
4. Indirect Object–Direct Object Constructions
   "Mommy showed *Daddy her new briefcase*."
   "I gave *Nikki my new toy* just to share."
   "Mrs. Gray *called me on her telephone!*"
5. Passive Sentence Forms
   "The car *was chased* by the dog."
   "My toy *was broken* by the hammer."
   "The page *was ripped* by a ghost, Daddy!"

Sound Production

Between ages four and five, most children become much better at pronouncing a variety of sounds. However, a number of children are still learning to produce some sounds even into the elementary school years. As a child care professional, being familiar with the ages for the development of various sounds will help you detect developmental delays and provide timely intervention for children in your care. With this knowledge, you'll be able to help parents know whether a child's speech development is proceeding normally.

Young children who have been learning two languages simultaneously since birth develop language mostly the same way as children learning only one language—but with a few differences. Bilingual children will speak their first words somewhat later. They may also blend parts of words from both languages into the same word, and they may mix words of different languages within a phrase or sentence. By age four or five, however, they recognize the two languages as separate and these "confusions" disappear.

Since most bilingual children are exposed more to one language than the other, they come to prefer one over the other. This may be because they feel more comfortable with it or because it's more effective in certain situations.

Cheryl is concerned about Angela's inability to pronounce the th *sound, and she asks about Angela's speech at the spring conference with Angela's teacher. The teacher shows Cheryl a chart explaining that the production of* th *is expected to develop in the seventh year. She reassures Cheryl that at this stage of Angela's language development, there is no need for concern.*

Communicative Competence

While young children are expanding their vocabularies and learning how to express their thoughts through oral language, they are also gaining *interactional* and *communicative competence. Interactional competence* is the ability to communicate effectively with others. *Communicative competence* means knowing how to use language and appropriate nonverbal behavior. It also means being aware of conversation conditions and rules. Here are some examples of communication behaviors in various cultures (Trawick-Smith 1994):

- Some Mexican-American children use touch and physical movements when talking with others.
- Some Chinese-American children use silence to avoid conflict or threatening situations.
- As a sign of respect, Brazilian and Peruvian children frequently say nothing to guests when they arrive.
- Arab children use silence to show they want to be left alone.

- Some Japanese-American children use a smile to hide embarrassment, anger, or sorrow.
- African-American, Puerto Rican, and Mexican-American children avoid direct eye contact as a way of showing respect for persons in authority.
- Japanese-American children and their families seldom touch others, particularly people of the opposite gender.
- Puerto Rican and African-American children generally stand close to the person they're talking to. They also use touch when talking with each other.
- Some African-American, Hawaiian, Puerto Rican, and Jewish families will all talk at the same time rather than speaking one at a time.

Cultural differences in communication and child-rearing practices tend to be context specific; that is, adults tend to prepare children for the types of skills they will need to survive in the particular society they're being raised in. The more aware children and adults are of these communication "rules," the better they are at communicating and the more comfortable they are in conversation in their culture.

Given how culturally diverse the United States is becoming, you may be working with families whose caregiving practices are very different from your own. Sometimes this may cause conflict. You can show cultural sensitivity by listening respectfully to concerns and by involving a family directly in resolving any conflicts. To succeed, you must try to understand caregiving practices that are different from your own or unfamiliar to you, and you must be willing to give them a try.

Thinking about such cultural issues and questions can help you look at and understand your own beliefs. Understanding how culture affects a child's development and learning can also help you appreciate the many different experiences young children have as they grow into adults.

In the next chapter on literacy development, you'll begin by looking at how children form an awareness of print. You'll learn specific ways adults can support the growth of print awareness in young children and how to recognize early writing behaviors. You will also learn why children need to see and hear written language to develop ideas about how to read and write. For many years, child development experts thought that reading developed before writing. Today, however, we recognize that children can learn about reading and writing at the same time *and* at earlier stages than originally thought. Finally, you'll find valuable information on the role of pretend play in promoting cognitive, language, and literacy development.

References

Hart, B., and T. R. Risley. 1995. *Meaningful differences in the everyday experience of young American children.* Baltimore: Brookes Publishing Co.

Trawick-Smith, J. 1994. *Interactions in the classroom: Facilitating play in the early years,* 317–322. Upper Saddle River, N.J.: Merrill/Prentice Hall.

9 Literacy Development

Reading and writing are essential tools in a literate society.

> Definition: *Literacy*—"the ability and the willingness to use reading and writing to construct meaning from printed text, in ways which meet the requirements of a particular social context" (Au 1993).

Unlike language, which develops naturally and rapidly during early childhood and without formal instruction, reading and writing evolves over a longer period of time. It happens quite easily for some children but it is quite difficult for others; most children need some kind of instruction to learn these skills. There is no specific teaching method that works equally well with all learners.

Learning to read and write requires more than cognitive ability; other influential factors include the following:

- physical ability (vision, hearing, small-motor development, perceptual–motor coordination)
- emotional interest (desire, interest, curiosity, motivation, confidence, enjoyment, perseverance)
- social support (encouragement, instruction, support, feedback)

It's important for teachers, parents, and others who work with and care for children to understand that individual children become literate in unique ways. It depends on the quality and quantity of their early language and literacy experiences and on the way they, as individuals, pay attention to and process information.

At ages four and five, when children typically enter education programs outside the home, they exhibit a wide range of literacy-related skills and abilities. For instance, in a group of five-year-old kindergarteners, some may have the literacy level of a typical three-year-old, while others may read and write more like an eight-year-old. Despite these wide differences, there are also some universal patterns in how children become literate.

Table 9.1: Signs of Early Literacy Development (Ages Four through Five)

Vocabulary and comprehension
Increases vocabulary, which improves comprehension
Acquires greater skill in both understanding and speaking language
Enjoys conversation with others
Learns to take turns in conversations
Enjoys rhymes, rhythms, chants, songs, and word play
Starts story-reading and book-sharing activities
Can fill in missing words or phrases during a shared book-reading activity
Can talk about and retell a story when given a little help from a teacher or other adult, or from looking at the storybook illustrations
Role-plays story characters and themes
Incorporates story characters and themes into pretend play
Incorporates story characters and themes into drawings and early writing
Can answer *who*, *what*, and *where* questions about a story
Print awareness and writing behaviors
Shows interest and increasing skill in reading public print, such as billboards, building signs, and so on
Says or sings the alphabet
Combines curving lines and letterlike marks with drawings
Attempts to draw or copy letters

Tries to write letters, even if incorrect
Writes in different directions on the paper (for example, vertically or right to left)
Recognizes and names most letters
Writes words in a string without spaces between them
Attempts to write letters; letter reversals are common
Attempts to write letters and numbers in order
Pretends to read
Writes familiar letters (though confuses upper- and lowercase letters)
Recognizes that groups of letters can form words
Makes first attempts at writing her name, including both upper- and lowercase letters
Starts to make distinctions between upper- and lowercase letters
Learns to write name using appropriate cases
Dictates labels and stories for art and other projects
Writes own labels and stories using developmental (or phonemic) spellings
May not follow left to right and top to bottom in early writing
Awareness of letter sounds and alphabet principle
Appreciates the fact that information and entertainment can be derived from print experiences
Tells others about ideas gained from reading and writing experiences
Develops a desire to read and chooses his own books

Awareness of Print as a Form of Communication

One of the first steps in literacy development is realizing that marks on a page can express a message. Children at ages four and five very closely watch the literacy-related actions of those around them, and they have a growing awareness that drawing and writing communicate ideas. As four- and five-year-olds encounter drawings and print in many forms and situations, they become more and more aware that the thoughts they have and share with others can be drawn or written down and read by others. This realization grows over a period of time. At the same time, small-motor skills such as hand-eye coordination are improving, making it possible

95

for preschoolers to begin to draw and write more accurately. In addition, their language development gives them names for—and ways of thinking about—what they want to draw or write.

Having paper and tools (drawing or writing) available encourages this process. Young children usually begin to draw about experiences that are meaningful to them. As they think about these experiences and represent them in their drawings, they often talk to themselves or with others nearby about their thoughts and what they are drawing. They may tell an adult what they want written about their drawing or use their own limited knowledge of letters to write out their ideas. In your work with children, you can help this process by saying, for example, "Tell me about your picture" or "Let me write down what you said." As children see their words written out by adults, they begin to understand that thoughts can be expressed not only through spoken words and pictures but also through writing. This is a huge discovery!

James, Cheryl, and Angela decide to celebrate James's pay raise by going out to eat. Some friends join the celebration. Angela becomes restless while they wait for their food. One of Cheryl's friends gives Angela a pencil and Angela begins to write lines imitating cursive writing on her paper placemat. Suddenly, she tugs at Cheryl's arm, points to her writing and says, "This says 'spaghetti.' This says 'milk.' This says 'salad.'"

Angela's behavior shows that she's beginning to understand how print is used to make a request. She has been thinking about what she wants to eat and observing others deciding what they want to eat. These decisions were discussed and then given to the server, who wrote down what each person said about the food they wanted to eat. Thought, oral language, and written language were all used to get what they wanted: food.

Ann and Jeremy are at a greeting card store in the mall. Five-year-old Jeremy knows it's close to Ann's birthday, and he tells her he wants to get her a card. Ann asks Jeremy how much money he has in his Mickey Mouse billfold. He tells her, "Four dollars." Ann shows Jeremy how the price is marked on the back of the card and helps him decide whether he has enough money. She

then shows him the section with birthday cards for mothers. Jeremy finds one he likes and checks with Ann to see whether he has enough money. Finding that he does, he takes the card to the cash register and pays for it. As soon as they get home, Jeremy goes to a basket on his toy shelf that holds pencils and felt pens. He picks up a red pen and writes "4 U" on the envelope. Inside the card he writes, "I ❤ U JEREMY."

Jeremy's behavior shows that he knows about cards and how thoughts are written on cards to help celebrate birthdays. He uses thought, drawing, and written language to convey his birthday greeting to his mother.

These two stories illustrate young children learning how to talk about and write down their thoughts. They also show how adults can support literacy development by helping children write their thoughts, by providing experiences for them to participate in literacy events (such as sharing letters, making lists, labeling, locating addresses and phone numbers), and by providing tools (paper and writing implements) for them to practice reading and writing.

As an adult, you can support young children's print awareness by doing the following:

- watching for opportunities for literacy development
- being ready to answer children's questions about reading and writing
- providing the time and the tools children need to read and write
- giving children as many opportunities as possible to experience many forms of literature through books, storytelling, plays, poetry and rhymes, songs, and drama.

Just as children need to hear oral language to learn to talk, they need experiences with spoken and written language to learn to read and write.

Just as children need to hear oral language to learn to talk, they need experiences with spoken and written language to learn to read and write.

Early Writing Behavior

At some point during their fourth or fifth year, most children begin to realize that drawings can represent objects and people, and that writing represents words for objects, people, or thoughts. Just as young children experiment with blocks and paint, they play and experiment with letters. Children's first attempts at writing can include imitating adult cursive writing as they attempt to write their names. Through such experimentation, children begin to learn the characteristics of written language.

As they begin writing, children make similar mistakes. For example, at first they don't notice that writing follows a sequence (left to right in English and right to left in Arabic and Farsi). Gradually, however, they internalize this rule. They also fail to realize that changing the direction of some letters changes their meaning and pronunciation. For example, reverse the direction of the letter *b*, and it's no longer a *b*. It can become a *d*, or even a *p* or a *q*. Physical activities, such as rhythms and dance that promote left/right concepts, as well as games that require the use of top/bottom, in front/behind, over/under, and other positions, all help children understand direction ideas in their "body" as well as in their "head."

Since writing is a complex task, it's also difficult for young children to think about what they want to write and how to make the letters that represent the sounds in the words, all while remembering details like leaving spaces between words.

The Alphabet Principle and Phonemic Awareness

Through instruction, children learn that there is a relationship between letters and sounds. By reading alphabet books, singing alphabet songs, and using alphabet puzzles and games, children become aware of letters, their unique shapes, and associated sounds. They also learn about the sounds of language through rhymes, songs, and storybooks. In fact, traditional nursery rhymes and other poetry help children learn to distinguish between different sounds. This ability to recognize that words are made up of individual sounds is called *phonemic awareness*. On the other hand, formal *phonetic* instruction, in which teachers use worksheets and repetitious memorization of isolated concepts, is not very useful at this age because this type of abstract learning is not only too difficult for preschoolers, it can be very discouraging.

Definition: *Phonemic awareness*—the ability to recognize that spoken words are made up of a sequence of individual sounds.

Early Reading Behavior

As with infants and toddlers, reading to and with young children on a regular basis is the most important factor in becoming a successful reader. Just as young children need to hear oral language to learn to talk, they need to see and hear written language to develop ideas about how to read and write. Young children who have had many experiences reading and being read to learn how to use books. They learn that a book has a front and a back and that the story does not begin on the title page. They learn about reading one page and then going to the next, and the general left-to-right progression of pages. While young children often say that the illustrations tell the story, adults can help them understand that the print actually tells the story. Reading to four- and five-year-olds also helps them better develop oral language by introducing new vocabulary words.

Equally important is the fact that children who are read to come to connect books with the enjoyable experience of sitting next to, or on the lap of, a caring adult and hearing wonderful stories. As children interact with books, they come to identify similarities between the stories and their own lives. For example, they can see in *Alexander and the Terrible, Horrible, No Good, Very Bad Day* that Alexander has bad days just as they do. They can also learn

> *Reading to four- and five-year-olds also helps them better develop oral language by introducing new vocabulary words.*

interesting facts from books, such as that a triceratops had three horns. They discover that books can provide information, comfort, and joy, and that reading can take them to new and fascinating places, both real and imagined.

Using books with repeated sound patterns and predictable text helps children become more aware of print. At first, many children think each letter represents a word, but they eventually discover that groups of letters represent words. Adults can help young children understand the relationship of words to the story by pointing with a finger to individual words as they read. Pointing also helps children observe the relationship between speech and print.

Because the illustrations in a good book support the text, young children soon become aware of text and how it works. When adults make comments and ask children questions while a story is being read, it helps children better understand what's happening in the story. Repeated reading of a book enhances children's understanding of the concept of *story line* (plot).

RELATIONSHIP BETWEEN READING AND WRITING

For many years, child development experts thought that reading developed before writing. Today, however, we recognize that children can learn about reading and writing at the same time and at *much* earlier stages than we thought. Four- and five-year-olds should not be expected to read and write like older children and adults. Reading and writing are complicated processes that take time to learn. Simply developing an understanding that there is a connection between reading and writing is an important first step in children's literacy growth. When young children have opportunities to write or to have their thoughts written for them, they begin to develop concepts about what a word is. Practicing writing their name, developing individualized vocabulary cards, and having adults talk with them about the letters in words, the letter sounds, and what words say all help children learn to read as well as to write.

Pretend Play

In general, four- and five-year-olds' play activities match their level of cognitive development. These are the peak years for fantasy and *sociodramatic* (pretend) play. These play activities usually involve a group of children playing roles and creating stories in loosely organized performances. The plays are based in reality and usually describe common events in children's lives, such as going to the store, making dinner, taking care of younger siblings ("You can be my baby brother!"), or going to the hospital.

Early in the preoperational stage, these plays are simple, basic, and easy to understand by adult standards. But as children's cognitive abilities develop, these plays include more and more information and more "actors." Generally, they are fantasies with a lot of dynamic, enthusiastic physical activity. Concrete objects are used to represent needed props to support the play's theme. Character roles are constantly changing.

HOW PRETEND PLAY AFFECTS SOCIAL AND EMOTIONAL DEVELOPMENT

Through pretend play, children are able to re-create happy events in their lives and deal with troubling ones, often acting them out in ways that give children a sense of power and mastery over people and situations over which they actually have little power. They can reconstruct these situations to achieve the goal or the ending they prefer. Pretend play also helps children understand other points of view in social situations. Interestingly, pretend play not only helps social and emotional development, it also promotes academic success in later years. Research on social-emotional and cognitive development shows direct connections between this kind of childhood social interaction and later school performance.

HOW PRETEND PLAY AFFECTS COGNITIVE DEVELOPMENT

As children create pretend worlds in their play, they are changing reality to fit their goals. This kind of thinking is the foundation for more mature reasoning and problem solving. In addition, play helps children improve their problem-solving abilities and creative thinking.

How Pretend Play Contributes to Language Development

To create a play, children must plan, discuss, and debate. This process gives them much-needed practice building communication skills. Through pretend play, children can experiment with and practice different kinds of communication: word use, phrasing, gestures and body language, listening skills, and so on.

How Pretend Play Contributes to Literacy Development

Using a variety of literacy-related props, children begin to use their new knowledge of print, writing, and reading. For example, the classroom pretend-play center may include a number of props with written words: storybooks, recipe cards, grocery-list pads, note cards and stationery, mailboxes, toy catalogs, TV guides, notebooks, message boards, and so on. These literacy-related materials can be included in any of the learning centers and used however children want. Experiences with such materials provide concrete opportunities to learn about reading, writing, and spelling.

Chapter 10 looks at the role nutrition and health play in cognitive, language, and literacy development. Some prekindergarten and kindergarten programs have expectations that don't take into account children's actual ages and capabilities, thus putting children at risk during their first school experiences. You'll learn why it's so important to have developmentally appropriate programs for young children and what those programs include.

References

Au, K. H. 1993. *Literacy instruction in multicultural settings*. Fort Worth, Tex.: Harcourt Brace College Publishers.

Factors Influencing Cognitive, Language, and Literacy Development

As noted in earlier chapters, the brain develops in response to individual experiences and is particularly vulnerable to certain types of experiences during certain periods of rapid growth. Motor development, first- and second-language development, math, logic, and musical learning are particularly important during early childhood years. This is a time when parents and child care providers need to be especially aware of children's senses, motor skills, and speech because, if problems exist, assessment and intervention are best done at the earliest possible age. Rich experiences such as music instruction, creative-movement opportunities, number games, and second-language immersion contribute vastly to the growth of children's brains and neurological systems.

Nutrition, Health, and Well-Being

As with infants and toddlers, preschoolers have continuing, though different, needs for sleep, rest, exercise, and nourishment. Even though many four- and five-year-olds are enrolled in prekindergarten and kindergarten programs, their need for predictable routines and an adequate diet is still very important. They also continue to need vigorous exercise and unstructured playtime. When these basic needs are not met, children have a much more difficult time focusing and learning.

Adult-Child Interactions

The types of cognitive-, language-, and literacy-promoting experiences children have during their preschool years influences later development. When children have limited or negative learning experience at home, then preschool or another early childhood program can offer important opportunities to increase their cognitive development.

Prekindergarten and Kindergarten Programs

Many children enter prekindergarten and kindergarten programs when they are between four and five years old. The demands on such programs are changing as federal, state, and local governments try to respond to the growing awareness of the importance of the early childhood years. Some demands are unreasonable because they require very young children to behave and perform as though they were older. In fact, expectations that don't acknowledge children's actual developmental level and age-appropriate qualities and abilities put many children at risk during their first school experiences.

As a child care professional, it's important to watch this trend because of its potential for both physical and psychological harm. Some school schedules created to serve the needs of older children fail to provide enough exercise, rest, refreshment, and nourishment for preschoolers. The exhaustion and stress connected with very busy schedules and performance expectations often lead to physical illness and behavioral problems in preschoolers. When children are scheduled as well for activities outside of school that leave little time for rest and unstructured play, their health and psychological well-being are put at risk.

When children are scheduled for activities outside of school that leave little time for rest and unstructured play, their health and psychological well-being are put at risk.

On the other hand, early childhood programs that *do* pay attention to the special physical and psychological needs of young children play a critical and essential role in their overall growth and development. These programs carefully plan for enrichment, and work to support children's growth, development, and learning. They provide links to professional services for parents of children with special developmental or learning challenges. In short, they work with families to ensure the best possible outcomes for each child.

Quality programs for young children meet accreditation standards set by professional organizations such as the National Association for the Education of Young Children. Accreditation standards address teacher training and qualifications as well as educational routines, nutrition, safety requirements, curricular expectations, and family involvement. Research by Dunn and Kontos (1997) on the effects of developmentally appropriate programs for young children shows the following:

- Children in classrooms in which their developmental needs were met scored higher on measures of creativity and original/imaginative thinking than children in academically oriented classrooms.
- In child-centered classrooms, children had better outcomes in language development and had better verbal skills than children in academically oriented programs.
- Where literacy environments were of high quality, children's receptive language was better.
- Children in developmentally appropriate programs showed greater confidence in their cognitive abilities and described their abilities in more positive terms.
- Most studies indicate that an "instructional" approach to teaching with young children is less successful than a child-centered approach.
- Children of low socioeconomic status attending developmentally appropriate kindergarten programs tend to have better reading achievement scores in first grade than children of a similar status attending kindergarten programs that are not developmentally appropriate.
- Differences between children in more or less appropriate classrooms often do not appear until a year or more later.
- There are emotional costs associated with academically oriented classrooms, particularly for children from lower socioeconomic groups and minority groups.

References

Dunn, L., and S. Kontos. 1997. Research in review: What have we learned about developmentally appropriate practice? *Young Children* 52(5):4–13.

The Role of the Early Childhood Professional

1. Give children individual and group learning opportunities that take into account their multiple intelligences, cultural backgrounds, and special learning needs.

2. Provide opportunities for language development that fit their special language needs and diverse sociolinguistic backgrounds:
   - Be aware of children's attitudes and responses to physical touch and personal space preferences.
   - Show appreciation for all languages and dialects.
   - Avoid criticizing or correcting children's language.
   - Encourage cross-language conversation.
   - Assist second-language acquisition.

3. Provide rich and varied experiences from which children can gain information and inspiration for language, writing, and reading.

4. Provide an intellectually interesting classroom that challenges but does not overwhelm children. Provide developmentally appropriate curricula and materials, routines, and activities. Adjust expectations to fit the age and individual needs of children.

5. Provide a language-rich environment where children have opportunities to talk with one another and with adults; where storytelling, book reading, conversations, and discussions are seen as important; and where writing is encouraged and supported.

6. Provide an environment that has many books, writing materials, visuals, and other items that grab children's curiosity and encourage beginning readers.

7. Provide centers and appropriate props and play materials that encourage pretend play.

8. Make sure that parents play an active role in their children's learning experiences.

Discussion Questions

1. Using Gardner's multiple-intelligence theory, create a special page about each preschooler in your care, identifying individual strengths and weaknesses. Are there any trends in the group as a whole? How might you adjust your curriculum to play to the strong points of the group while strengthening the weaknesses?

2. What activities and materials do you currently include in your program that help expand a preschooler's vocabulary? Are there activities or materials you could add to your setting that might strengthen the children's awareness of oral and written language? Try implementing one new activity in your setting, and then monitor its impact.

3. Chapter 8 discusses how communication styles sometimes vary by culture. Have you noticed communication style differences among the children in your care or among their family members? In what ways do you acknowledge and show respect for these differing communication styles?

Further Reading

Coles, G. 2000. *Misreading reading: The bad science that hurts children.* Portsmouth, N.H.: Heinemann.

Gauvain, M. 2000. *The social context of cognitive development.* New York: Guilford Press.

Göncü, A., and E. L. Klein. 2001. Children in play, story, and school. New York: Guilford Press.

Greenspan, S. I. 1997. *The growth of the mind and the endangered origins of intelligence.* Reading, Mass.: Addison-Wesley.

Neuman, S. B., C. Copple, and S. Bredekamp. 2000. *Learning to read and write: Developmentally appropriate practices for young children.* Washington, D.C.: National Association for the Education of Young Children.

Puckett, M. B., ed. 2002. *Room to grow: How to create quality early childhood environments.* 3rd ed. Austin, Tex.: Texas Association for the Education of Young Children.

Schickedanz, J. A. 1999. *Much more than the ABCs: The early stages of reading and writing.* Washington, D.C.: National Association for the Education of Young Children.

Tabor, P. O. 1997. *One child, two languages: A guide for preschool educators of children learning English as a second language.* Baltimore: Brookes Publishing Co.

Other Resources

- American Speech-Language-Hearing Association
  10801 Rockville Pike
  Rockville, MD 20852
  800-638-8255
  www.asha.org

- Association for Childhood Education International
  17904 Georgia Avenue, Suite 215
  Olney, MD 20832
  301-570-2111
  www.acei.org

- Board on Children, Youth, and Families
  The National Academies
  500 5th Street NW
  Washington, D.C. 20001
  202-334-1935
  http://www7.nationalacademies.org/bocyf/
  For more information on Howard Gardner's theory of multiple intelligences, go to http://www.newhorizons.org/strategies/mi/front_mi.htm

- Reach Out and Read National Center
  29 Mystic Avenue
  Somerville, MA 02145-1302
  617-629-8042
  www.reachoutandread.org

- Voices for America's Children
  1000 Vernon Avenue NW, Suite 700
  Washington, D.C. 20005
  202-289-0777
  www.voices.org

- Schaefer, S. and Cohen, J. 2000. *Making investments in young children: what the research on early care and education tells us.* Washington, D.C.: National Association of Child Advocates. Available at http://www .voicesforamericaschildren.org/Content/ContentGroups/Publications1/ Voices_for_Americas_Children/ECE1/2000/eceinvest.pdf.

Index

Other Resources from Redleaf Press